Rebel Woman

Baring My Battle Wounds and Learning to Love the Scars

Michelle Margaret Marques

Copyright © Michelle Margaret Marques

All Rights Reserved.

DISCLAIMER

In her memoir, *Rebel Woman,* Michelle Margaret Marques does not apologise for anything. She writes the book with love in her heart and takes responsibility for everything she needs to. The chapters in this book reflect carefully chosen parts of her story and the lessons she has learned along the way. The advice in the book is based on her views and represents how she healed and developed herself. Michelle accepts no responsibility or liability whatsoever on behalf of the consumer or reader of this material. She does not suggest you should follow her advice to a "T" nor does she guarantee specific results. Any negative perception of anyone is entirely unintentional. Michelle cannot be held responsible for the use of the information provided.

This is a book of memory, and memory has a way of telling its own story. I have done my best to make it tell a truthful story.

Each chapter in this book is the author's present recollections of experiences over a lifetime. Some of the names and characteristics have been changed to protect the identity and privacy of their families. Some events have been compressed, and all dialogue is given from recollection only.

All rights are reserved. No part of this publication may be reproduced, distributed or transmitted in any form or by any means, including photocopying, recording, or other electronic or mechanical methods, without the prior written consent of the author or the publisher. Except in the case of brief quotations embodied in critical reviews and other non-commercial uses.

ISBN: 9798692715180

Imprint: Rebel Universe Publishing

Connect with Michelle at
www.michellemargaretmarques.life

CONTENTS

DISCLAIMER 3
FOREWORD by Nancy Florence 7
Rebel Woman Introduction 9
Chapter 1 My sexual abuse 11
Chapter 2 Giving birth at 16 20
Chapter 3 The Day I Took My Life into My Own Hands 26
Chapter 4 My Nana Slipped Away 30
Chapter 5 My Mum Is Gone 35
Chapter 6 My Family breakdown 41
Chapter 7 A Series Of Unhealthy Relationships 44
Chapter 8 My Papa passing 56
Chapter 9 Never Having Family Support 59
Chapter 10 Attempted Fraud 62
Chapter 11 Going to Prison 70
Chapter 12 My Brother Slowly Killed Himself 77
Chapter 13 My Marriage Breakdown 83
Chapter 14 Journey to the new me 86
Chapter 15 Claims of Sexual Abuse 90
Chapter 16 The Friendship I Paid For Dearly 101
Chapter 17 My Children 108
Chapter 18 Raising four children alone 117
Chapter 19 Not Knowing My Granddaughter From Birth
.... 121
Chapter 20 Father or Not 123

Chapter 21 Always Feeling Alone 126

Chapter 22 Being Strong And Finding Strength Is The Same 129

Chapter 23 Myself First.. 131

Chapter 24 No Mask to Hide Behind, The Freedom of Vulnerability and The Courage to Own It All......................... 135

Chapter 25 Desire to dream and achieve 138

Chapter 26 My Business Life 140

Chapter 27 My Mission... 145

Chapter 28 Delicious discovery year... 147

Chapter 29 Becoming the Rebel Woman.................................. 150

Thank You... 153

Acknowledgements.. 154

Notes and Insights.. 156

FOREWORD
BY NANCY FLORENCE

Look at *this Rebel Woman*!

Look closely...and you'll see yourself.

Rebel Woman is a modern tale of the most powerful cornerstones of a woman's life.

Michelle left no stones unturned. She covers abuse, loss, life, death, and everything in between.

You will nod a lot, have tears come to your eyes...and at times you'll find yourself smiling softly.

Michelle meant every word she wrote in this book. She is one of the bravest women I know, and I've learnt so much from her.

And by the way, (this is for you ...the reader) when she tells you that she loves you —she truly means it.

She wrote this book for you. So, make yourself comfy and soak in all of the love that is infused in this book.

You'll be reminded that you are not alone.

Whatever you are going through, she has been through it, or a version of it.

Michelle has all the scars on her back and yet she is a beautiful example of joy and femininity for all of us.

This book will help you get your innocence back.

Michelle is one of the rare human beings on the planet who has maintained a child-like innocence and happiness.

She has been through hell and back, but she still loves herself, and she loves people.

In fact, she loves YOU.

Nancy Florence

Life & Business Coach

Rebel Woman

Introduction

I am Michelle Margaret Marques, born Michelle Moffat in Glasgow to Scottish parents Margaret and Joseph. I grew up on a Glasgow council estate. It wasn't easy and we didn't have a lot of money, but we were surrounded by a large and loving family who were fiercely loyal to each other (for the most part anyway). Oh, they could be just as cruel to each other as they were loving and loyal. However, the love and devotion always outweighed any other aspect.

My mother came from a Catholic background and my father a Protestant background. It was difficult growing up with that mixture of backgrounds in Glasgow, and I was often beaten up by both sides just for being who I was. I was taught that I should never back down, I should never show fear, and I most certainly should always stand up for myself and stand my ground even if my head was being kicked in— and I did and still do. I grew up strong, no matter how horrible it may sound or seem to have been. Although I didn't know it or even begun to understand it then, my childhood taught me every lesson I ever needed to build the life I was destined for. A destiny that is far more important than the turbulence I endured. I attribute that background to the iron backbone and sheer resilience I pride myself on having now.

A champion cannot help but do what they were meant to do. It's the drive to do what one is good at. Despite the turbulence of my journey, I believe I have lived on a course

I felt drawn to. A life that has driven me to fully engage in my purpose; a life that only I could uniquely accomplish.

I believe I was given a predestined purpose, a drive for the contentment of a life well lived and the rewarding task of acting on my gifts.

Throughout this book, I am going to take you on a journey of handpicked pieces of my life, which will give you insight into the woman I am today—my grit, determination, and fierce authenticity—and how I got there.

I should warn you that some parts of this story are graphic and will shock you. My intention here is to be raw and authentic and at no point has anything been included for shock value. You may feel emotional, and I hope that you allow yourself to feel that emotion and embrace this journey with me.

I hope that this journey will awaken the champion in you too.

Chapter 1
My sexual abuse

The Little Girl That Has Never Given Up Fighting!

This story began in 1984. I was ten years of age, and I was sexually abused by my cousins' grandfather; a man who lived in the block of flats next to ours.

I was coming home from school for lunch one day, which is something I didn't often do and therefore, my mother was not expecting me. Mr Aganue, my cousins' grandfather, shouted to me from his window and asked if I would run to the shop for him. I agreed and made my way up to the third floor to go get the money and find out what he wanted. When I arrived, his door was slightly open. Despite knocking, he didn't answer at first, so I opened the door a little and called out for him. 'Come in', he shouted in a deep and impatient voice that made me feel on edge. I went inside, and when I did, he closed the front door and locked it behind me. I remember feeling slightly unsafe but didn't think much of it at the time. I noticed that there was newspaper all over the floor in the hallway and found it strange but didn't give it much more thought until after.

I don't quite remember how he approached me or what he said at first. All I remember is that after he locked the door, he sat on a chair at the bottom of the hallway, then he pulled me over to him. As he began touching me, he said you don't need to be afraid, I was scared, I felt paralysed with fear. I didn't understand what was happening, and I could never begin to imagine what was going to happen next. He pulled me towards him and began to take down my tights and underwear. I remember he said, 'you are so small, and I find that very nice'.

He bent me over in front of him and spread my legs, he then began touching my vagina and spreading it open, he kept saying it looked adorable, and he liked it. He started putting his fingers inside my vagina and saying that it was tight, and it felt perfect. He continued putting his fingers inside me for a while, making comments about how good it felt and how nice it looked. He then attempted to put his penis inside my vagina, and it wouldn't go inside. He kept trying, and he wasn't happy that he couldn't get it all the way inside. It was so painful. I was so afraid, and I was crying. In a sharp angry voice, he said, 'be quiet I want to enjoy it'. He tried again and again, but it just wouldn't go inside.

He sat back on the chair, pulled me to the floor, and told me he wanted me to kneel in front of him on the newspaper. He got hold of the back of my head and grabbed my hair tight, pulled my head down and put his penis in my mouth. He then pulled my head up and down by my hair frantically. Enraged, I was gasping for breath, gagging, and crying. He continued to do this until he ejaculated in my mouth. When he let go of me, I was gagging and spitting the sperm out. He kept telling me to make sure it went on the newspaper. He then pulled up my underwear and tights gently, told me it was our secret, and I shouldn't tell anyone. He gave me twenty pence, opened the door, and told me I should go straight back to school because I was late, and I would be in trouble. As I was walking out of the front door onto the veranda, he said, 'remember don't tell anyone about this; it's our secret. You will get in trouble'.

Although my house was in the next building, I ran back to school as quickly as possible, trying to forget what had just happened, let alone make sense of it. I was so confused. I didn't know how I should feel or what I should do. At first, I told myself to just forget it and that at least when school was finished, I could go get some sweets with the money he had given me. Buying sweets like that was a bit of a luxury. And I guess that was the only way I could try to deal with what had happened. I didn't understand any of it and certainly didn't know how to start.

Nevertheless, something inside me felt...sick. I kept spitting. I couldn't get rid of that taste in my mouth. all the way to school I kept spitting and spitting. No matter how hard I tried I couldn't forget it, and I couldn't stop the sick feeling or that taste in my mouth, even when school was finished. I felt so awful that I didn't even bother to buy the sweets I thought might distract me. I went home and went to my room without having dinner. My mother came to my room. In a slightly concerned but caring voice she asked, "do you want to talk about what is wrong'?

'Nothing is wrong. I just don't feel well', I said. This of course was very true, but of course I couldn't explain why to her, because at that time I didn't understand.

The next morning, no matter how hard I tried, I could not put this out of my mind. I could not stop feeling sick. His voice ringing in my mind telling me it was our secret, and that I would get in trouble. I knew inside something wasn't right, and something was telling me it was him that would be in trouble, not me. I was also feisty back then too, and there was never any trouble I didn't handle or was I afraid of. I was taught to always stand up for myself and to never back down and at that time, I had an immensely loving and protective family. Especially my grandmother, who absolutely adored me. She was someone I could go to for anything. We always had a voice in my family. Sometimes we had to shout to be heard, of course, but we always had a voice.

So instead of going to school, I went to my grandmother who lived on the next street over. When she opened the door and saw me standing there, she immediately knew something was wrong. I didn't know how to tell her. I don't even remember what I said to her; I just blurted it out as best I could, looking to find some sort of answer or some understanding. My grandmother held me and said very gently, 'this is not your fault. You could never be in trouble for telling anyone and I'm glad you had the courage to never keep this a secret'.

At that point I stopped feeling so sick and stopped focussing on that taste in my mouth. Although what happened would never be okay, I felt better at that moment, and I knew I had done precisely the right thing. In some ways, I'm glad that experience happened to me at a time in my life when I didn't fully understand the gravity of it. My grandmother handled this with such care and grace. She told no one at first, and she and I went straight to the local police station. Her primary concern was to take care of me with as little outside influence or fuss as possible; while at the same time having this officially logged as soon as possible. Had she told my family before the police picked him up, all hell would have broken loose and my uncles would have killed him.

I remember having to wait at the police station in the reception for a very long time. They didn't seem to take it seriously. We were eventually taken into a very white room with stark lighting. It was an incredibly uncomfortable setting. I was interviewed with my grandmother present, and I tried my best to answer the questions and give as much information as I could make sense of at that time. I didn't know how to explain some of the things that happened or how it made me feel; I was ten. It seemed like these questions went on forever and were repeated again and again. My grandmother was frustrated and annoyed because it became increasingly clear to the both of us that the police weren't taking it seriously. We waited a long time after the interview. I was then taken to another starkly, brightly lit room where a doctor examined me and performed a vaginal examination. This was all too much for me and very confusing. This was another man putting his fingers inside me, and I was now being told this was okay. I was so traumatised by this that I don't remember much after the physical examination. However, I clearly remember the doctor telling my grandmother that although there were signs of vaginal interference. Because actual penetration didn't occur, there wasn't enough evidence to prove he had done this to me. Now, as an adult, I'm appalled that he would take such a narrow-minded view and be so quick to conclude that there was not enough evidence. The police proceeded to charge my perpetrator with sexual abuse, however, after a court hearing, they never gave him a custodial sentence.

After some time, I moved on and continued with my life, trying to put that incident behind me. At age seventeen, a point where I thought I had forgotten it (and I mostly had), my cousin admitted to my uncle that my perpetrator had been abusing her for years. Her experience haunted me from then on and I felt responsible somehow. If I had done something sooner, there would be more evidence. If I had fought him at the time or screamed until someone heard, they would have caught him. I would have been taken seriously, and he would have never been able to do that to anyone again.

He may have picked the wrong person when he picked me because I was never going to stay quiet, and he actually took a significant risk in doing so, but he picked me at the right time for him to still get away with it. He chose the right person when he picked her because she was just the right kind of quiet and awkward. She always sat in the corner reading a book. Everyone always thought she was just weird and pretty much ignored her—although we understand now why she was the way she was. She came forward at precisely the right time for the law to take her seriously. Plus, this was now the second report against him, and they had to take it seriously. I was also re-interviewed, and he was charged for both accounts of sexual abuse. A more significant trial started at that point, and we gave evidence via video link. The newspapers began reporting about it, and a couple of other women came forward who had lived in his building when they were younger. He was sent to prison. I can't remember the exact details, but it was roughly a one year sentence reduced to a few months because he was in his seventies at that time. I remember walking down the street one day and suddenly freezing when I saw him walking towards me. He had been let go, and I didn't know. I will never forget how paralysed I felt in that moment. It was like being right back in that house when I was ten. He died not very long after he was released from prison, which I remember at the time was a great relief to me. I felt he had finally gotten what he deserved now.

My cousin and I had many conversations after that and the details we shared helped us both over time. I began to see that I did what I was meant to do, and I was not responsible for the authorities not taking me more seriously. I remained faithful to the feisty person within even then. In fact, if I hadn't have come forward it may have been much worse for her and they may not have taken her seriously either. Over the years, I've dealt with the trauma as an adult. I've managed to forget a lot of the details of those conversations. However, there is one in particular that will never leave me. My cousin told me she can't put milk in tea because it reminds her of sperm. Imagine what it was like for her feeding her baby on a daily basis.

It only happened to me once, and I am thankful that I had the strength to tell my grandmother and that I knew I had a loving place where I had a voice. Despite this, for a long time, I felt guilty that I had the strength to stop him from ever coming near me again, and she didn't—a "survivor's guilt" of sorts. I understand we are different people, she wasn't as strong, and more to the point didn't have a voice or such a loving place where she could come forward. Her side of the family was not as warm. In fact, I am convinced on some level they knew what was happening, but that's not my story to tell.

I thank myself for being the strong person I am and have come to understand that we are all responsible for ourselves when the day begins and ends.

Although I suffered a lot through that ordeal, the suffering I put myself through later on was in some ways much worse and had far-reaching effects on my adult life. In my relationships, I always felt insecure. I never felt really loved or safe. I always felt very uncomfortable about sex and conditioned myself to just put up with it., to go through the motions as a normal thing that happened between two consenting adults. Although I could rationalise why I felt that way, I could never let go and really enjoy it. It took years for me to deal with the after-effects of this coming back up in my adulthood and in some ways I relived it in every new relationship and intimate encounter I had. Until I truly unpacked it, I didn't realise that I needed to forgive the ten-year-old girl inside me that I thought had let me and everyone else down. I needed to let go of the thought that the feisty fighter had abandoned me right when that little girl needed her the most because she never abandoned me, she was right there protecting me all the way. I needed to make peace with what I did or didn't do in those moments where I blamed myself for allowing him to do that and understand that I probably did the very thing that kept me safer than I could have possibly been if I had put up a fight or screamed. I needed to learn to truly love myself and appreciate that I was still lovable. Finally, I needed to understand it for what it is. It's no better or worse than it is; it just is. It forms part of my story. It's no longer part of me or takes up any power in my life. I am the only one responsible for giving it power, and I choose not to.

I feel it's essential to give you a sense of how much it took for me to write this; the sheer fear I felt sitting down to begin this chapter because I didn't know what was going to come up and how I was going to feel about it all. It's also crucial to let you know how writing it made me feel at specific key points and the sense of relief and fearlessness I now feel having gotten to the end of that piece of my journey. Because as much as it is essential to tell the story, it is just as vital to give you a complete view of the emotions and a window into who I am and how I deal with the journey I have had early on in life. It's also important because I want to give you strength in knowing you can overcome the effects of anything if you look inside, genuinely love yourself, take power back for yourself, and choose to see it as just part of the story.

When I started to write my fingers began to get cold. When I started to get into the details of what happened, I began to feel uneasy and my stomach began to churn. The more information poured out the sicker I felt, and at one point I actually thought I needed to be physically sick. I wanted to stop writing but at the same time I wanted to write more. I have known from the beginning that this chapter was going to be one of the hardest to write and in many ways, it has kept me from writing this book sooner. When I was giving the raw and graphic details, I felt cold; physically in my body and psychologically in my mind. This is very likely the central nervous system's way of dealing with it. Surprisingly I didn't cry during the details of the actual abuse, but then again it isn't really a surprise to me because I made a decision a long time ago never to give any tears or power to that incident again. Once again, my feisty fighter protected me just like she always does.

I did cry three times during this chapter, in fact (make that four now) and that was when I began to write about how gentle and caring my grandmother was and how going to her made me feel better immediately. I also cried when I was talking about forgiving the ten-year-old girl inside. In many ways, I still carry her with me, but I choose to bring her courage and fierceness with me these days. I also cried when I began to explain how I felt a sense of fearlessness reaching the end of writing that piece of my journey, and I have to say I feel the same sense of fearlessness now having wrapped up Chapter One.

Chapter 2
Giving birth at 16

So, I really thought things through before having sex for the first time. I had been dating my boyfriend since I was fourteen and we planned everything properly, waiting until my sixteenth birthday to have sex. After all, sixteen was the legal age in the UK, and it felt right to do it properly, so to speak.

We used protection, and everything was fine, or so we thought. Except five weeks later, I found out I was pregnant. That was definitely not part of the plan. I planned to go to business college the following January and have a career. At no point did I even consider the plan to include a baby.

I was freaking out when I found out. I was terrified. I thought my mum would kill me for sure. I really didn't want to have to tell her. Somehow, from somewhere I summoned up enough courage to speak with her and to my surprise, she didn't kill me (obviously). She didn't shout or scream. She didn't cry, blame me, shame me, or throw me out the front door—all of which I had imagined in my mind over and over again. No, instead my mum was the most amazing, understanding, and surprisingly calm she could have been. She told me how disappointing that was for sure, but that didn't change the fact that she loved me and would support me 100%. This conversation with my mum actually became one of the most amazing I ever had with her. I still draw strength from it today and cherish every word. If it hadn't been for this one conversation and this incredible life-changing situation I found myself in, my life may have been very different. I owe a hell of a lot in my life to this conversation.

In this conversation, with a powerful yet caring tone my mum said, 'this doesn't have to change anything you want to do with your life, it just alters the path, it may slow you down, but it won't stop you. You can do anything you put your mind to. You were meant for more. Just because you were born in a council estate in Glasgow does not mean you were meant to stay there. You were born for more than this, for bigger things, and you can do anything you want'.

I still remember every word as if it was yesterday. I should have every word memorised because I have played that conversation over in my head thousands of times, and I draw strength from it each time life throws a curveball. I pick myself up and get on with it. Or get up, dress up and show up as I say now. My mum also told me that she was pregnant with me when she was sixteen, and she didn't have the support of her family. She ran away with my father until I was born, and she didn't want the same negative experience for me. She had wanted to become a designer for wedding invitations and me being born changed that. She never did accomplish that and she didn't want that same unrealised potential for me. I feel so honoured that my mum had learned so much from her experience and come through life with the ability to have such care and support. I was grateful she was able to pass on her lessons and change the outcome for me.

Her lesson to me may have been too late to prevent my teen pregnancy. However, it was the most life-changing lesson I have ever had in breaking the cycle of adverse outcomes. She said, 'you will call the college tomorrow and explain. You will defer your start date for a year. You will have this baby and you will go to college'.

I knew her tone of voice all too well, which meant there was no argument to be had. 'I will look after the baby while you go to college', my mum said with a reassuring smile. 'I want you to enjoy it; go out with your friends and be a student'.

My mum is my superhero. She took care of my son and gave me the kind of support I could have only ever dreamed of. I am the person I am today because of her understanding, belief, and support. I wouldn't even be alive without her.

I bet there were some preconceptions when reading the title of this chapter. The usual story of a teenager who had an awful time being pregnant and giving birth and no family support. If you made that assumption, you were mostly wrong; except for the nearly thirty hours of excruciating pain in labour. Thankfully my mum was with me the whole time. She refused to let them give me an emergency c-section because my son's umbilical cord was around his neck, the labour was taking too long, and he was becoming distressed.

Mum ordered the delivery team, 'no! Give it a while longer. He can do it'.

She was right. He was born soon after, but he was blue and it didn't seem like he was breathing. Several doctors rushed into the room in a frantic commotion. No one told me what was happening. I started to panic and think he was dead. Then suddenly he let out this cry. He spent the night in the critical care unit but he was healthy. The midwife, however, was not so understanding about teen mothers. She was borderline nasty to me in delivery. Before she left, she actually said to me in a cold manner, 'I'll see you here next year'. A heartless, judgemental woman...but I digress.

Giving birth to my son changed my life in many beautifully surprising ways and in some tough ways as well. It changed me as a person. It gave birth to my new life and made me more driven for a better future than I had ever been before. It had given me the responsibility for another human being who relied on me for everything. Of course, at times it felt like way more responsibility than I wanted or could cope with. However, it made me determined to give him a good life and all the love I had inside me. It changed the course of my life forever, and I would not go back and change a single thing because it made me the person I am today.

I am so grateful the universe chose me to live that experience early on in life. Both the universe and my mum knew I was the right person for the challenge and the lessons I was meant to learn. I'm even more grateful that I got to give my mum the gift of a grandchild; the only grandchild she ever knew. If I hadn't gotten pregnant at sixteen or had the courage to see it through she wouldn't have had the joy of having a grandchild.

My mum died at the age of thirty-seven when my son was just twenty-six months old. I am grateful the universe gave me the biggest challenge of my life so early; for her and for me. Those three years between me getting pregnant and my mum passing away were the closest we ever were. I am beyond grateful that we got to share so much during that time, a period in my life that I cherish. It was a challenging time but beautiful as well.

You will learn the full story about those years as we go through this book, however, I want to give you some perspective on the magnitude of challenge and beauty of life itself. I was pregnant at sixteen and gave birth to a healthy son just under three months before my seventeenth birthday. I almost died when my son was six months old. My grandmother died two months before my eighteenth birthday, and my mum died ten days before my nineteenth birthday. The most important women in my life now gone, I was a single mum with a twenty-six-month-old son and a family that fell apart. Now, I was on my own with no real support and no real love outside of my son.

The stability I knew at that point was gone; my life changed again presenting me another grand challenge. My superhero and biggest supporter had gone and my world turned upside down. My mum was in my life for such a short time; it felt like it was gone in a heartbeat. However short I had her in physical life, she is with me always and everything I ever needed from her she gave to me—every bit of love, every lesson, every belief in who I am—she made sure I had it.

I am devastated by her loss, and I wish she got to see my life grow and my other two sons and my daughter. I wish I could still share precious moments together, however I know she's not truly gone. I know she watches over me from my head to my toes, and she walks with me everywhere I go. I talk to her every day, and I know how deeply proud she would be.

I want you to know, no matter how tough or how painful the challenge or heartache may be; you are enough and you will get through. You may or may not have someone giving you fantastic support or teaching you valuable lessons. Just know the universe sends you everything for a reason. You may have manifested it from negative thoughts or experiences or you may have manifested it from positive thoughts and feelings. No matter how it came into existence in your life, it's yours to own, and you have one of two choices: own it like the beautifully courageous person I know you are or let yourself be a victim of it. I know which one I chose and I also know which one has the hardest road to travel. Ultimately the choice is always yours. Choose wisely and be strong. I already know the decision you'll make.

I don't even know you personally yet, but I love you still.

Chapter 3
The Day I Took My Life into My Own Hands

(Literally)

This day started just like any other. Except unbeknownst to me, it was going to be one of the most life-defining days of my entire existence thus far, and might possibly still be many years later.

I woke up with my then six-month-old son needing a feed and a cuddle. A big smile greeted me, and we snuggled for a few minutes before feeding, bathing, and dressing. It was a lovely day, and that evening my son was sleeping over at my mother's; a rare chance for me to relax and get some rest, and for my mother to spoil her only grandchild at that time.

What I didn't know was that my evening was going to be anything but relaxing. This was the night I almost died at the hands of someone who was meant to love me. Someone who was meant to protect me and be my best friend—the father of my son.

It began as a usual argument. He was angry that I would not comply with yet another demand from his mother and he hit me with a shoe. Lots of things went through my mind in just a few seconds. *Is this really going to be my life?* I thought. *Is this really what I am going to accept? Is this the life I want for my son?* I had so many questions and every single answer was 'no'.

This was not the first time he had been violent. This was the third and in that moment I decided it was going to be the last. No more chances. No more begging to come back, pleading and crying, manipulating and controlling. It wouldn't get to the point where he would be on his knees again in tears, making me feel like the terrible one. This was not going to be my reality anymore, and I was ready to stand up for myself. I knew I didn't deserve this. I knew I was worth more and I definitely knew how to fight for myself. My very being was a product of fighting for myself and standing up for myself. It had been woven into my DNA growing up, and I wasn't about to abandon that part of me now.

At that moment I made one of arguably the most stupid, non-rational decisions I had ever had to make (but I would say it was actually one of the best). I hit him back with the shoe. Yes, I could have done a whole host of other things like walk out, call the police, lock myself in another room, go to a neighbour, or go to my mother's. But I am a fighter and I did what fighters do. At that moment that was the right decision for me, and I take responsibility for my part in what happened next. And by the way, I do not advocate this as the right decision for anyone else in the same situation.

So, after I hit him back with the shoe, he hit me with a glass bottle. He then knocked me to the floor and began kicking me over and over. All I could do was curl up in a ball and try to protect myself as much as possible. I laid there while I was violently assaulted by the person who was meant to love me the most, while thinking about my beautiful six-month-old son, thankful he wasn't there at the time. All I could do was hope I would actually see him again let alone cuddle him.

I want to pause for a moment and let you know that if you have or are experiencing violence in your relationship—that person *does not love you*, and *you deserve a million times more*. Please hear this loud and clear. If I could, I would lovingly shout that from the rooftops so you could hear me.

He kicked me until he ran out of energy or anger; I suspect it was both. He then left me there on the floor and ran out of the house. He had no idea if I was dead, alive, or dying, but he left me anyway. This person *did not love me*. He didn't even care enough to get help, make an anonymous call, or take any action at all; he just disappeared. I was left unconscious, and I don't quite remember, but I was likely unconscious all night. Thankfully my next-door neighbour came knocking on the door the following morning. After hearing all of the shouting and screaming the night before she knew something was wrong. She made her husband kick the door in, and they found me on the floor. They called an ambulance and my mother was told that due to internal bleeding, I could have died if I hadn't gotten to the hospital in time. They estimated I had one hour to live when I was brought in. I spent weeks fighting for my life. Now I was a fighter for real, and thankfully, I still am. I was left with broken and cracked ribs, a dislocated hip, a busted up face and body, and I couldn't walk properly.

The good news was I recovered fully and I never took him back. I never gave space for the crying and begging again. I never spoke to him again until my son was ten years of age. I broke the cycle. I won the biggest fight of my life. I put myself through hell, but I came out the other side victorious and stronger, and I actually thank myself for having the courage to make the decision I made. I knew it would result in him beating me. Of course, I didn't think he would beat till I was nearly dead. I couldn't have predicted that, but I literally took my life in my own hands that day and it was one of the best decisions I ever made.

No one on this planet has the right to put their hands on you. I don't care what you said or did. No one should ever accept or endure one moment of violence, especially from someone who claims to love you. If you take one thing from this chapter, even if you have never experienced violence, I hope you know that you are a human who deserves to be treated with love and respect. You are beautiful, you are worthy of love, you are lovable, and you are enough. Never accept any less than you want or deserve from anyone, no matter how much they profess to love you. Love is shown in actions of care, respect, and kindness. Anything other than that is *not acceptable*.

I may seem like I'm this badass warrioress (which I am), but it took me a long time—even after standing up for myself and winning the biggest fight of my life—to understand deep down that I am beautiful, I am worthy, I am loveable, and I am enough. It took me a long time to accept responsibility for my actions that night and to stop being a victim of what happened. What happened is now just part of my story, and I use it as fuel to thrive. I took my power back that night. However, I didn't really claim my power as my own until many years later, and I don't want that for you!

Whatever is causing you pain or causing you to accept a victim state of mind or situation, claim it now, take your power, flip your hair back, and walk away into owning your life and your decisions. Own it all *now*.

I don't know you, but I love you still.

Chapter 4
My Nana Slipped Away.

August 1991, my grandmother (Nana) passed away peacefully in her sleep after a six month battle with cancer. That battle was incredibly difficult for me. My grandmother was an amazing woman and a massive influence on my life. She also taught me I could have everything I wanted because she often gave it to me.

Sadly, I actually stopped visiting her a couple of months before she died. For a long time, I didn't like admitting that to myself, let alone the world. I was ashamed of those choices and I deeply regretted missing out on those precious times. I didn't know at the time she was dying because she didn't want her grandchildren to know. In hindsight, had I known I would have spent every moment I could with her. I stopped seeing her because of how sick she was. Skin and bone, at one point she weighed just over 60 lbs. and she could hardly speak. I just couldn't cope with how upsetting it was and how it was affecting her, so I hid from it and pretended it wasn't happening.

The day that she died, I was at work and I couldn't focus. I felt something was wrong; something deep down didn't feel right. As I searched inside for what the answer could be I got a powerful feeling that I had to go see my nana. This feeling hit me like a bolt of lightning; it was so intense. I knew beyond a shadow of a doubt I had to go, and it had to be now. I went into my boss' office and attempted to explain what I was feeling. I didn't understand myself let alone how to make sense of it for someone else. So, I just blurted out, 'I have to go now. I have this unexplainable feeling that I have to go see my nana, and I don't care if you fire me'.

I'm not sure if she was more shocked by my blabbering or that I didn't care if she fired me, she looked at me wide-eyed and then said, 'okay, you go if you have to'.

I got to my nana's house as quickly as I could. I was expecting the worst by the time I got there because the feeling I had was so strong. When I got there, much to my relief and surprise, she was resting in the chair in the sitting room, looking better than she had in months. She was talking properly, and we sat and chatted for hours. I sat on the floor in front of her while she brushed my hair. She always loved to do that. Every chance she got she would have me sitting on the floor while she brushed my hair for a hundred strokes—her own secret method for healthy, shiny hair. It was always almost certainly more than a hundred strokes, and I have a sneaky feeling it was her way of spending time with me (either way, I had great hair and a great bond with my nana; a win-win). 'I am so sorry I haven't been to see you', I said as she pressed her brush through my hair. 'I have missed you so much'.

'It is fine', she said gently. 'You have nothing to be sorry for.

'I love you so much and I should have been here'.

She looked at me with that look that she always had, like nothing I could do would disappoint her. 'I love you too. You were right where you were supposed to be'.

Although I didn't know it then, that was our last conversation and the last time she would ever brush my hair. That was our goodbye, and a most beautiful one at that.

For a long time, I thought about what I should have said that day, what I would have done differently, what I would have told her, and how I should have stayed longer. If I had known, it would have been so different, and of course, it would have, but not in the way I was trying to convince myself. It was beautiful just the way it was, and it happened just the way it was meant to. Now, I'm incredibly grateful for the sublime bliss of the unknown and for the joy of that afternoon, just sharing time with her in love and normality. When the end came that is precisely what she wanted.

I was back at home, around 10 p.m. that same day, when there was a knock at the door. Immediately I knew something was wrong. That intense feeling I had in the morning was soon back and I rushed to get to the door. It was my uncle David who confirmed my worst feeling without even saying a word. He came inside, and we all sat down with my mum, and he broke the news. My nana had passed away peacefully that evening.

I had never experienced such overwhelm of emotions, thoughts, and grief all at one time. At that moment, my life changed again; another challenge of who I was deep inside and another battle to overcome. At that time my nana was the most important woman in my world. I didn't know how I was ever going to get over her loss. I had not experienced much loss at that point in my life, but her death was one I felt so deeply I didn't think I could possibly survive.

I later came to realise she and my mum were the two most important women in my entire life and they both gave me so much that I could never have gotten from anyone else. My mum was never the same person again; a part of her died with my nana. I think my mum's heart was quite literally broken after the loss of her mum. Until she passed there had never been a day where my mum didn't see my nana. The lessons of the past had taught them both, life was too precious to miss. My mum and my nana had missed out on valuable time before when my mum was pregnant with me. Just as I had somehow known to go see my nana that day, my nana was there the day I was born, sitting by my mum's bedside when she woke up from an emergency c-section. My mum never understood how my nana knew to be there. The connection and bond I experienced with both my nana and my mum is incredible and I would have given anything to have had it for so much longer in my physical life. However, I still carry the strength of those bonds, and I always will. The love, the lessons, and the relationship they shared with me and showed me how to have enables me to share that with my children, my friends, and my clients. It is quite simply what gives me the capacity to share so much of myself and it makes me an incredible coach.

Pay attention to the bonds you have in your life and the love you share. Life isn't always perfect. Life sure as hell isn't always easy, but you can choose how you survive it all. You can choose any moment as something to be cherished, beautiful, meant to be, and something to help you thrive. Or you can select the same moments and label them as painful and let them destroy you one moment at a time.

Choose life, live life, be joyful and live in love and cherish every single moment you have on this planet with every person you love or have loved. Although they won't always be there in your physical life, the memories, the moments, the bonds, and the love will always be with you. I have lived through more death and pain over the years that it almost doesn't seem real. Sometimes when I look at my story, it seems like more than anyone could endure in two lifetimes. People I know have asked how I am still sane (who knows if I am?), how I'm still standing, and how I can always give so much of myself to others.

My answer is: because I can. I can do anything I put my mind to, and I do. I give because I can. I love because I can. I show up in this world the way I want because I can!

You can do it too.

I don't know you, but I love you still.

Chapter 5
My Mum Is Gone

But She will Always Be with Me

My mum died in 1992 ten days before my nineteenth birthday. She is my hero and is still the most significant influence on my life today and always will be.

My mum was one of the most beautiful human beings that ever walked this Earth. She was a beam of light and love, always smiling and laughing. She had a big open smile, warm and inviting, and had an infectious laugh. She had love for everyone and would have done anything for you. She was always singing and had a wonderful voice. She played all kinds of music—everything from country music to reggae, but Elvis was her favourite. She listened to his music and watched every movie, interview, concert, news report, and anything else regarding the man.

My mum died of heart failure at thirty-seven-years old. It was so sudden and unexpected. I believe my mum died of a broken heart. As much as she loved her children and the joy we brought her, she never recovered from losing my nana. She died exactly fourteen months after my nana. It's a day I will never forget. The events that took place that day are forever etched into my mind.

It was early in the morning. I was getting ready for work and there was a knock on my door. I thought it was the postman. He actually had a habit of hand delivering my mail. I was in a rush that morning and annoyed that he would knock on my door. I remember thinking, *that bloody postman, I don't have time for you today*, as I stomped down the hallway. I opened the door forcefully in annoyance, and much to my surprise my uncle Patrick and my papa were standing there. Now I knew something was wrong. Everything inside me knew something was off but I didn't want to believe it for a second. My mind was racing trying to make sense of it, to find a rational explanation. Why were my uncle and papa at my door so early, especially since I lived about fifty miles away from them? They were wearing heavy rain jackets, and would often go fishing at Loch Lomond which wasn't too far from me. My brain decided that must be it; they came to have a cup of tea before they went fishing. So, I asked them about it but my uncle said, 'no we came to see you'.

Now my fears were confirmed. Something was definitely wrong. 'Let's go sit down. I need to tell you something'. We went into my front room, and he sat me on the chair, and he kneeled down in front of me. My heart was pounding just like it is now as I'm writing this. I began to shake in anticipation of bad news. 'Your mum died at 5 a.m. this morning'.

I'll never forget those words. 'How could you say such a thing'? I asked, clearly in shock. 'You can't say things like that and I then got up and walked away.

But my uncle got hold of me and sat me back down. 'She's gone, Michelle. I would never just say that to you. She died this morning, and I had to come and tell you. We're going to go see her in the hospital. I'm going to take you to see her. You get ready and then we'll go'.

I remember I didn't cry. I went into my bedroom and stood there looking in my wardrobe for something to wear like it was a typical day. From that point on, I would never have another ordinary day again.

Soon, we all got in the car. During the hour or so drive no one really said much of anything. We went to the hospital and saw her. I still didn't cry. The doctor said he tried to revive her several times, but she didn't respond. I thought she probably didn't want to come back and I was angry in a way for her leaving me and my son. How could she do such a thing? I was numb. I can't explain the feeling of complete disbelief and shock. My mind simply couldn't accept it, and was trying desperately to adjust to this new reality. In fact, I didn't cry for a few days. It didn't feel normal—I didn't feel normal. Later that day I went to the pub with my uncle Patrick, just the two of us.

We talked about her and shared each other's disbelief. We had a few drinks, and my uncle confided, 'you are the closest thing I have to my sister now'. I cherish that time with my uncle in those hours trying to accept that she was gone.

The last time I saw my mum was just a day and a half before she died. My son was partially living with her at the time while I got myself on my feet after my father kicked me out of the house during an argument. We would usually get together on a Monday evening for dinner, and I would see my son. I wasn't feeling well that Monday, so I cancelled. She was so adamant that she wanted to see me and make sure I was okay that she made my father drive her out to see me. She didn't often make him do anything, let alone something he didn't want to.

When she arrived, she brought me some food and Lucozade, which she always gave her kids when we were ill. It's one of those crazy family remedies (we all have them). We sat on my bed and chatted, and when she was satisfied that I was actually okay she went home. Tears are streaming down my face right now as I write this. I didn't realise at that time just how significant that night was going to become in my life, just a mum fussing over her daughter, but in retrospect it was much more than that. It was the last time I ever saw her, the last time I would ever speak to her, the last time she would ever hug me or tell me she loved me. As I reflect back on that night I wonder if deep down she knew she had to see me, just like I knew I had to see my nana. Over the years I've come to believe she did, and I now realise that was her way, yet again, of making sure I knew I was always cared for and always loved. That's what she has left me with after all these years. I always felt seen, heard, and loved and that is what I want to give to those I love.

I hear her voice every time I have a triumph, every time life throws me a curveball, and in the music she loved. I feel her warmth every time I hug my children. I see her every time I look in the mirror; she's right there looking back at me saying, *I love you and I'm so proud of you.* I am incredibly grateful that I still hear her voice; her words of encouragement and belief in me.

I have learned over my lifetime that there is beauty in everything; you just have to be open and willing to find it. Sometimes you have to look hard, and I am grateful I have learned to do that (though it took a bloody long time to do so). There is even beauty in death and in pain, but you have to heal the pain. The beautiful yet painful thing about the loss of someone you love dearly, is that while they are no longer physically present in your life, they are in everything you do and everything you are. They are always around you. You will always have them within you. You will always carry their love everywhere you go, and they will still influence you. Cherish your moments with those you love now, but remember they are still with you when they are gone.

My life is still full of the beauty she gave me and the sheer drive and belief she instilled in me. Both her loss and her influence motivate me to become more every day. She taught me to be me and to go after everything I want with everything I have inside me. My life is lived fully because of her and the magnitude of her loss makes me want to live the life she always knew was possible for me. I live life for me, but I do it in honour of her. She wasn't with me long enough, but she gave me everything I ever needed to take me through this life while she was physically with me.

I encourage you to focus on and work toward bringing the beauty with you in your life from each person that you have lost, and from every other situation of pain. Even in the worst times, there is still some beauty. Ultimately, it's your choice, but by doing this you'll, heal your pain from your present and past and live in your life in greater harmony. Live life your way, with your love.

I want to share with you that this was one of my most painful chapters to write and in many ways, I kept putting it off. I sat down to conquer this chapter several times, and the resistance defeated me until today. Then I realised that if I didn't write it today, it was still going to be holding me back and denying me the feeling of freedom through my vulnerability. I had to conquer the fear of feeling whatever was going to come up and get it done.

I gave you everything inside me today. There were moments of sadness and moments of joy in remembering, especially the love she gave my son. There were times I had to stop and just sob. I also smiled and laughed, and at times I didn't know what I was trying to say (thanks to my editor for helping me tidy it up a bit), but I wrote until it felt complete. I hope it inspires you to live the life you were destined for. Don't ever let anything hold you back. Lean into it, feel all of it, and bloody do it with everything you have inside you.

I don't know you yet, but I love you still.

Chapter 6
My Family breakdown

I am sure you would agree that the death of a mother in any family has a massive impact. Every family deals with it in their own way, some better than others. It's likely that the families that deal with it well are the ones who are already close and have a strong enough bond. That wasn't the case in my family after my mum passed away. Our family literally broke down piece by piece. My mum was the glue that held us all together. She was the reason we were a unit at all because we all fell apart after she was gone. The typical family I had grown up in ceased to exist overnight, and we now had sheer hell in its place.

My father hit the bottle hard. My brother began running around getting wasted and my sister was also running wild. I had my son to take care of. We were dealing with each other full time again and the loss of my mum in our own way. We all grieved independently of each other. We didn't grieve together, and we certainly didn't speak about how we felt or about my mum. It was almost as if she was never there in the first place in some ways, yet there was a massive void at the same time. It's really hard to get your head around and in a lot of ways the loss of our family unit took more healing than the loss of my mum.

I remember a newspaper article was once written about my life because I had achieved a lot in the community. I talked about my mum in that article, about her influence on my life, and how amazing she was. It was a good article and one I thought my family would be happy with. But no, they were not pleased I had spoken about my mum in a newspaper.

They were angry about it. My sister was livid and practically threatened to drag me all over the front garden at my father's house. She was screaming and shouting at me, 'how dare you speak about my mum in the newspaper'. Anyone would think I had said some terrible things the way she was reacting. These are the kind of messed-up incidents I had to deal with. There was always some kind of drama or argument. It was continuously draining and not a healthy environment to be in, let alone conducive to healing a significant loss.

At one point my sister and I physically fought each other, which resulted in me being rushed to the hospital with sliced feet, from knocking over glasses and standing in the glass while we were wrestling each other. I was so enraged I didn't even know I was standing in the broken glass barefoot. I had gashes that narrowly missed my main nerve to my little toe.

There was another incident when my father came home from the pub and began arguing with my sister and put his hand through my glass door. There was a lot of anger, pain, unresolved grief, and we all took it out on each other in various ways. Some of us took it worse than others. Although I never set out to cause hurt or heartache, I put all of my anger into whatever was thrown at me.

My boys grew up in this hell and they were very affected by it, especially Michael. When he became a father, he decided to take my granddaughter away and keep her away. I tried to get away, and we moved several times to keep our distance from the drama. It was never far enough, though, and it didn't seem to make a difference how far we moved; the tension always followed. I would run away, but it wasn't until years later, when I finally realised the only way I could have the life I wanted was to cut them out completely. I had tried everything else up to that point, and it hadn't worked. I was always trying to make a better life, running my business and living in the right area. Making sure my boys went to a good school and we could travel. Yet always felt I was being dragged backwards with each step I took forward. The more I tried and achieved, the more drama I attracted from my family. It got to the point where I was simply drowning. I finally had enough, and we moved down south, far away from everyone.

You will be faced with choices in your own life. To get what you want for yourself you will need to make some tough choices. You may have to cut some people out of your life, including those who you grew up with. You are not responsible for the decisions of others or their behaviour. However, you are responsible for your choices and your behaviour. Take ownership of your actions and make choices that are going to serve who you want to show up as in the world. Be bold and courageous enough to make the choices that affect your life in a positive way. Don't ever allow anyone to infect your life with negativity and pain— even if it's family.

Be you, do you, and don't accept anything less than the standard you want for yourself.

I don't know you, yet, but I love you still.

Chapter 7
A Series Of Unhealthy Relationships

After a world of pain and suffering, feeling like I was in the same relationship over and over but with a different person; who was the common denominator? Me, of course, and I now take full responsibility for my part in it all. I still hadn't healed me, but the first step in that healing process was accepting responsibility for my part in it, owning it, and not being a victim to it.

I was always a victim because I made myself one. I attracted that into my life over and over again, until I healed and took back self. Taking back self is one of the critical elements of healing along with taking ownership of your part in all of your suffering. Before I learned that I put myself through a lot of pain; some of which you have already learned about.

A good deal of that pain included my string of relationships, some unhealthy and some extremely harmful. You will also notice a pattern, as I eventually did, and that the model gets better as I heal and take back self. With each experience I realise I grew and got clearer on my standards and what I wanted. You will also see it didn't happen quickly. The universe will keep teaching you the same lesson until you learn it. I appear to have been a slower learner back then. But I hope by sharing my process, you can either avoid your own unhealthy patterns or stop them more quickly than I did.

You already know about the most extremely unhealthy relationship I was in, so no need to cover that again.

However, it still forms the model. It's the very thing that instigated the pattern. After I promised myself, I would never be in an unhealthy relationship again and no one would ever treat me like that again, I still did it. However, I'm going to throw you a little curveball in here.

The next relationship I got into wasn't the unhealthy kind you would expect. We met after my mum died and although I didn't realise it at the time, I was utterly broken (high functioning but still broken). I was sending out a subconscious SOS because I needed someone to look after me. We attract what we want, good or bad. This situation was no different. I was drawn to him, not because I was physically attracted to him, but because he was a safe bet as I came to realise much later on. We don't always consciously make the connections at the time, and we often make choices without truly understanding the reasoning behind them.

This man was kind, gentle, a bit of a nerd, and didn't have very much experience with women. He was besotted with me and absolutely out of his mind with pride to think I showed interest. I liked that and I needed it at the time. He was blind to the fact that I was almost broken (or maybe he didn't care). He also attracted what he wanted. He was very loving and giving but I couldn't give it back. I got pregnant quite quickly, something his mother was absolutely against. He adored me and he would have given and done anything for me—and he did.

I was now the taker in this relationship. He was filling up my cup so much and making it so easy for me that I didn't have to give much back. I couldn't give much back anyway because I didn't have the capacity for it at the time. But I needed to take it because I didn't have any love for myself. I wanted affection from him when I wanted to have it. When I didn't want it, I didn't want him anywhere near me. I could have walked right over the top of him if I had wanted to and I probably did to some extent, except I didn't want to be that person. I knew this relationship wasn't healthy for him or me, and I had told him so. I told him I wanted him to have the kind of love he felt for me with someone else, and I wanted to feel that kind of love for someone.

I wanted more (sounds crazy doesn't it). I had a man that adored me and who gave me everything and I wanted more. However, what I wanted was to feel more. I wanted to feel crazy love, passion, and a deep connection. No matter how much I tried and wanted to feel the same for him I just couldn't. He wasn't that person to me. He was my safe bet; the one that took care of me while I tried not to rebuild myself.

Despite my honesty, he wouldn't accept it. We had my son Michael by that point and he was determined to make it work. He fought hard to show me he loved me and that we could be happy. He tried and tried, but the more he did so the more I couldn't feel what I needed to and wanted to. It was an unhealthy place for both of us. I soon began to feel empty all the time and thought there was something wrong with me. I felt as if I wasn't meant to be happy or to have a fulfilling family life. I'm sure he felt insecure and empty like he wasn't enough and there was something wrong with him.

Nine months went by after I had initially told him how I was feeling about the relationship. All that time, we were putting ourselves through pain, unhappiness, and guilt before I finally got enough strength to end it. It was horrible. He begged me to keep trying, but I knew I had to finish it for us both. He said I destroyed him. He moved away and didn't see his son. I found out years later that anyone new in his life didn't know he had a son. For a long time, I carried that guilt with me; the thought of putting him through that much pain made me feel like a selfish person. But I eventually learned it was the best thing, the kindest thing, for us both. Otherwise, we would have only destroyed each other.

Looking back I had love for him, and I was deeply grateful that he was there for me when I needed someone to look after me the most. But ultimately I'm glad I realised it was unhealthy and had the strength to end it for us both. I learned a lot about myself, I healed a bit more, I grew, and most of all I have a beautiful son from it.

My next relationship happened quite quickly after that, too fast, and I learned a valuable lesson—be careful what you wish for.

I wanted crazy love, crazy passion, and insane connection. And I got it...but I should have definitely been clearer about everything else I wanted in a partner. He was everything my previous partner wasn't—full of confidence and a bit of a bad boy. He even drove a sports car...that he eventually crashed upside down into a ditch. We instantly connected and we were together every moment we could be. He stayed at my place every night.

He would go to work and come straight back to mine. It was full-on head over heels. We were consumed by each other and I got pregnant quite quickly; another pattern that continued. I couldn't get enough of him and it made me blind to the faults and the traits I should have avoided. He was the broken one this time. He would drink way too much, but of course, I didn't see that. We had a lot of passion, including when we would argue, and we started to disagree a lot after I got pregnant. I had a miscarriage, and as painful as that was, it brought us closer. We agreed we weren't going to have a baby now. We were going to take our time a little more. Except the universe (or my son) had other ideas and a few weeks later I found out I was pregnant again. What can I say? I told you it was passionate.

The cracks kept becoming more visible as time went on. He crashed his car and I began to notice just how much he drank. His father even harassed me about allowing him to drink so much. He was a grown man, hugely built at 6'4" man and no one allowed him to do anything. He did what he wanted. I found out he was taking drugs when he went out with his friends. Turns out he had always been taking them here and there.

Soon, the abuse started. It was mental abuse at first— name-calling, putting me down, criticising how I looked, my weight. I would tell him I was going to end it if it didn't change. 'Who is going to want you? You are just a fat cow with three kids. No other man is going to want you', he would say from time to time.

For a time, his abuse worked. I was back there again, wrapped in guilt for leaving my last partner, believing there was something wrong with me. That I wasn't meant to be happy or meant to have a fulfilling family life. And I sure as hell didn't feel important or loved. I began to believe relationships weren't for me; I wasn't good at it, I wasn't meant to be in one, and I wasn't meant to be happy in one. I gained strength from that in a way, and I decided if I wasn't going to be in a happy relationship, I wasn't going to be in any. I knew I didn't deserve his abuse, and I knew I didn't want it for my sons or me.

One night during an argument, he grabbed me by the hair, dragged me across the floor, and spat in my face. In that moment the fighter in me rose up. There was no way in hell I was going through that again, not for a single minute. I picked up the phone and called his mother, told her exactly what had happened, and told her to come to get him and his things. She came straight away. She had already been telling me before this that as much as she loved her son, I deserved better and she was right. That was the end of that, right there and then.

My son Michael went through hell after that breakup. He had come to see Liam's father as his own and actually called him Dad by his personal choice. As much as my ex welcomed that at the time, he didn't want it that way after the breakup. Stephen wasn't so affected; he hadn't ever bonded with him that much. Daniel only wanted Liam; he was cruel. He would come to pick Liam up and wouldn't even acknowledge Michael (his way of hurting me). Michael would call out after him as he walked down the path to his car, and he wouldn't look back. It was heart breaking, Michael would be screaming, 'I want my daddy', over and over. You have no idea what it is like to sit and try to explain to a three-and-a-half-year-old that isn't your daddy, and you can't go with him. The heartbreak is unbearable. I stopped him from coming to pick Liam up because it was just too painful for Michael. His grandmother would pick him up instead. Eventually, Michael stopped asking for him. I picked myself up, I lost a lot of weight, I started my own business, and I built my life with my sons on my own.

I decided yet again I wasn't meant to be in a relationship. I was much better on my own, and now I had more evidence and a new belief to support that. It was safer to be by myself; no one could hurt my sons again. No one could hurt us again. There was no way they would get attached to someone, and no way someone was going to walk away from them and cause pain. Of course, I realised much further down the line I was probably protecting myself more than I was protecting them. I spent almost thirteen years on my own raising my sons. That's how much protection I believed we all needed. I didn't want anyone else in their life, and I wanted their home to be safe. I wanted it to be their place of security, where they knew no one was going to hurt them or leave them again. Sure, I dated here and there, but nothing serious. I didn't let anyone close enough. No one ever met my sons, and no one ever came to my house.

This also brought on a series of unhealthy relationships, including being raped by someone who was meant to be my friend. And a couple of other attempted rapes too—casual relationships that were abusive or where I was being used in one way or another. However, my home was safe, and my boys had security. That was our safe space, and that's what mattered. During this time I also dated someone in New York. We were friends to begin with, and in a lot of ways he was my rock. He pushed me to achieve more with my business and be more assertive as a person. 'The quiet little girl from the UK', he would call me (clearly he didn't know me as well as he thought). This man still has a lot of influence on who I am today. I loved him so much, but he didn't have the capacity to love me the same. As much as he represented stability for me—I could talk to him about everything, and he was emotionally supportive of what I wanted from my life—he wasn't emotionally available in any other way. He had had a hard time trusting because of experience from his previous marriage.

I spent eight years trying to be everything I thought he wanted me to be—most of the time feeling insecure, trying to prove myself to him, showing I wasn't like her, trying to get his love and heart, and ultimately going through a rollercoaster of inner turmoil that eventually almost took my emotional wellbeing from me. The relationship, on the one hand, was a great support system for me and on the other was emotionally draining. In reality, it was terrific, and it was unhealthy in equal measure. He cheated and he told me; I forgave him, but it didn't matter. I never felt genuinely secure, and I never felt emotionally loved. He would never say, 'I love you', only 'that's why I love you' or 'I have love for you'.

Once again, I began to wonder what on Earth I had to do to be happy in a relationship, to be loved and have a fairy tale ending. Despite this, his influence pushed me to be stronger, it forced me to be more confident, and pushed me to be surer of who I was and what I brought to any relationship. He didn't put me down or try to abuse me. He told me to be me and do what I wanted to do. As I stepped more into who I was becoming and taking back more of self, I stopped trying to prove myself to him. I stopped trying to prove myself to me. I began to realise there was nothing wrong with me after all, he just didn't have the capacity for me, my love, my strength, my passion and my drive. It wasn't me that wasn't enough. He never believed or felt he was enough and I can say that because we remain friends even now and he has told me.

I have come to realise that's why he pushed me so much. That was his way of showing love. That's what he had the capacity for and made him feel valued and worthy of me. It took me almost a year to decide to end things. It was one of the hardest decisions I have made, I knew I was never going to get the relationship and the love I wanted, but I didn't want to lose my friend. Something else happened that ultimately made me end this relationship, and I wanted another child, (yes, I know) a baby girl. I kept having these images, visions, call them what you want, but to explain I kept seeing this baby girl around two years old. She had big brown eyes and lots of curly hair. I spoke to him about it, and I told him I think she's meant to be mine. He would say he wanted a baby but only someday. At one point I finally posed it to him, 'we aren't getting any younger and we have already known each other for eight years'.

As I was getting stronger in myself, I was growing tired of the delaying tactics and lack of genuine commitment. These images were now getting stronger and the feeling stronger as well. It was confusing to me that I wanted to have another baby while having these surreal images, but it was real. A friend drew this little girl as I sat and explained what she looked like in my mind. In the picture, it was so evident that this was precisely the image I had been seeing. I soon ended our relationship and thankfully, at least for a time remained friends.

I wish I could say that was my last unhealthy relationship but alas—we have one final ill-fated romance to explore.

I met my daughter's father in August 2010 after I was starting to rebuild my life. It began with a spark, and we soon became inseparable. I also got pregnant quite quickly (see the pattern again). We decided we would make a go of it and we moved in together. This was now the first time I was living with someone after almost thirteen years and also the first time my sons Michael and Liam were now sharing me with someone and having to try to accept someone else's rules. It wasn't easy and neither my boys nor him took to the adjustment kindly.

Let's say there was a constant battle of ego and male dominance that went on between them. They didn't like each other. My husband was trying to assert dominance, and my boys were far from accepting. Neither side behaved well and I was in the middle. My marriage was very unhealthy, not because of physical abuse or even any real mental abuse but because I felt emotionally tortured. There was no intimacy, no affection, and barely any communication. I would try to talk to him, but he didn't want to listen. He would dismiss my emotion, roll his eyes and say, 'oh this again', and tell me I needed to draw a line in the sand and move on. Sometimes he would completely ignore me; he would sit and look right through me. It didn't matter if I was calm, angry, crying, or anything; he would simply ignore me. This emotional turmoil was slowly destroying my wellbeing. The anger I felt inside was eating me alive, and it was affecting everything else around me. However, I stayed, and I dealt with that for almost four years. We didn't even sleep in the same bed for the last two years. I kept telling him I was going to go if it didn't change, but he didn't care nor was he willing to change anything. I asked to go to therapy and he refused. I cried myself to sleep many nights.

I laid there wondering why I just wasn't good at relationships and why I kept ending up in unhealthy, unhappy relationships. What had I done that was so wrong. I was torturing myself, trying to figure out why he was putting me through this. I went back to my dear friend, the one I had inside who told me I wasn't meant for relationships, and this time I had more than enough evidence that I was better on my own.

Finally, I had enough. I knew if I stayed, I was going to lose myself and become emotionally broken. I wasn't going to allow that now, after everything I had come through. This savage, this fighter inside me wasn't about to give up now. Instead of attempting to figure out why he was doing this to me, I had grown enough to know I had to figure out why I was doing this to myself. Why I was accepting this level of behaviour. Why I didn't love myself enough to put myself and my happiness first. Then it hit me. I asked him to leave and he wouldn't, so I found somewhere else to live. With each relationship, no matter how unhealthy, came the lessons, the beauty, the scars, the strengths, and the gifts. I believe I attracted each one for many different reasons, but most of all, they all came to teach me my worth, my strength, my capacity to endure and love. To show me I am unbreakable and I deserve everything I ever wanted—I call them Stephen, Michael, Liam, and Caragh. They are my heart, my life, and my soul. I would go through everything again ten times over to have them.

It's been over four years since I left my last relationship, and in that time, I have done a lot of unpacking, healing, and personal growth. I have continued to put myself first and I always will. I am happier now than I have been in my entire life. I have learned all of the lessons I was meant to learn from unhealthy relationships. I can say that with strength and absolute certainty because for the first time in my life I've stayed alone because I wanted to do so. I wanted to do the work it would take to heal, to learn, and to get clear on what I want from a relationship and what will and won't work for me in my life now.

I am thoroughly happy alone. I love my life and I love myself unconditionally. My turning point came when I learned to fall deeply in love with myself and accept all of my edges and imperfections. I'm more confident than I have ever been. I am unbreakable. I have learned that no matter what I will always be okay, and no one can ever change who I am in my core. I am loveable, I am worthy, and I am enough.

I'm sure you have seen distinct patterns in my many mistakes. However, you can also see clear trends in my growth. Each time I was getting stronger. Each time I was learning more. Each time I valued myself more, found more worth, fell more in love with who I am, and took back a bit more self.

Take back self, love you, be you, do you, and don't ever accept anything less than you are worth.

I don't know you yet, but I love you still.

Chapter 8
My Papa passing

You haven't seen me describe any positive male role models in my life so far, and this may not seem like the place to do it. However, my grandfather (papa) was precisely that kind of man—especially in later years after my mum passed. He worked away a lot when I was growing up, but when he was around he was a significant influence. The things that make me smile when I think of him were his booming voice and his great character. He was a disciplinarian a lot of the time and was very serious about teaching us right from wrong. My papa was a stringent Catholic and had very high morals. He was a very proud man who always worked hard and provided well for his family. He cared deeply about how he was viewed in the community and did not like any of his family being at the centre of questionable behaviour. He could be hard at times, but deep down he was a softy.

At times, of course, I really disliked how hard he could be. In some ways, I was scared to let him down or get in trouble. He really hated us speaking Glaswegian (Glasgow) slang, and whenever he caught us, he would correct us and make us repeat it the proper way. It annoyed the hell out of me back then; now I am so thankful for it. It's mostly because of that influence that I can express myself in a way that is understandable to anyone and feel confident in any social setting.

After my mum passed away, my papa was practically the only constant in my life. He was always at the end of the phone for advice or support. Whenever I went home to visit, I went back to his house. Up until he passed away, I went home as often as I could. I took him on holiday to Jamaica for his birthday one year, and he protested about me paying for it the entire time. I'm so thankful I could do that with him. I couldn't have known then he wouldn't be here much longer—only around two more years. He had been feeling down and lonely for a while before he passed away. I'm sure he was still struggling with the loss of my nana and my mum. My grandparents were together for over forty years. I also think he had been drinking a little too much whisky. He had come through a triple heart bypass, and he was dealing with diabetes. However, overall, he was in good health—strong as a bloody ox. Nothing much could keep him under the weather for long, that is for sure. And he looked great for his age. He was in his seventies and didn't look a day over sixty.

He passed away, one-night peacefully in his sleep. He was in the home and bed he had shared with my nana with her picture right beside him. It is my belief he decided he had been here enough, and it was now time to go back to her. This was another significant loss for me. I had lost the last constant influence in my life. The grief hit me hard and, in some ways, it sent me on a spiral of emotion. Three of the most significant people in my world were now gone. I felt like I had no one left. I now felt alone and deeply lonely. His funeral was tough for me, and I didn't stay long at the wake. I went back home to my life to figure out how I was going to deal with having no significant people in my life.

I still miss him a great deal, though the influence he had in my life will always be with me. I miss his loud voice and his big laugh. I miss him holding me to a high standard—a standard I now hold myself to. Thank you, Papa. You and your strong influence on my life will always be remembered and appreciated dearly. Your constant presence will still be missed. I love you.

I have learned a lot from life and in some ways a lot more from death. There is one thing that will have a lasting impact and make the most difference in your life—that is practicing being truly present. Present in your day to day life, with your loved ones, in your conversations, and in any situation that holds any kind of importance to you or those around you. Live fully in every moment and soak up every detail you can, no matter how insignificant it may seem at the time. Those are the moments that you will search your mind for when the time comes. The moments that will carry you through anything with comfort, joy, and love. Be present in everything and in all ways.

I don't know you yet, but I love you still.

Chapter 9
Never Having Family Support

And How It Made Me Stronger

Have you ever felt like in your search for a better life, you weren't fighting strangers and enemies but the people who you knew and know you the best? If so, we have a lot in common. Pretty much my whole family (not just my immediate family) never believed in my dreams. They never thought it was possible. They thought I couldn't do what I wanted to do and that I was living in the land of the cuckoo— that my hopes and dreams would never happen. They believed that a young woman from my background, with no real financial support, could even begin to achieve the kind of things I wanted and the things I have done.

My whole life they've made comments like, *you have forgotten where you come from*, and, *you think you're better than what you are*. They would actually try to talk me out of things I wanted to do, tell me it would never work, and I should just get a job and be happy. It goes deeper than that, though. They would delight when things didn't work out for me. They would actually say things like, *she's fell off of her pedestal*, and, *she fell flat on her face again*.

When I got a lovely house and car, I was told you don't need those things (even though I could afford them). When I took my sons on holiday or bought them good things, I was scoffed at and told that they just need love. When I worked hard, I was told I shouldn't be working all the time and should be at home with my sons. These comments also influenced my sons, and they would sometimes have the same attitude. I was laughed at, slagged off, put down, and pretty much became the joke that everyone talked about.

I spent a lot of years angry, hurting, and trying to prove myself that it didn't matter whether or not I did well. My family's influence was cracking my tough veneer a bit. To them I was just a big joke who kept chasing a stupid dream. When I went from project to project, they accused me of scamming. If I travelled a lot they thought I was drug trafficking. When I had success, they would say it wouldn't last. Pretty soon I just stopped telling them anything. It didn't matter to them and it was less fodder for them to chew.

After some time, I stopped trying to prove myself to anyone. I learned there was only one person I needed to prove anything to and that was me. I had known from the start what I was capable of, and I had done enough to prove to myself what was possible. I learned to love myself, and I loved myself enough to never give up. I stopped being angry, which was the best thing I learned from them. It took a while but another valuable lesson I learned from the whole experience was that I was stronger than I knew and even more so than my family gave me credit for. It taught me that I could endure anything in business and still thrive.

My family's lack of belief and support was downright cruel at times, but it didn't break me. It gave me ovaries of steel, an iron backbone, and every tool I needed to survive the successes and the setbacks. Going through such a constant battle of self with my entire family watching for my demise has taken me to a place of inner strength that is entirely unbreakable. I have managed to rise above it all and never quit.

Not a single member of my family has ever bought a product that I make or have sold. They have never paid for treatments in my spa, nor have they ever bought a ticket to one of my events or workshops. You don't need to worry about the outside world when you are constantly challenged by those within. The good thing that comes is sheer fearlessness. I no longer worry about launching a product or service because there is no longer any criticism that I cannot handle. I've also learned that your tribe is out there. There are people in this world who will support you and be there for you if you just put yourself out there.

Go out there and get yours, whatever it might be. Don't let anyone discourage you no matter where you come from. You were meant for more.

Go find your tribe and just bloody love yourself enough to keep trying, no matter how many times you have to do so. Get up, dress up, and show up.

I don't know you yet, but I love you still.

Chapter 10
Attempted Fraud

A series of bad choices and mistakes set me on a path of what could be seen as self-destruction. However, it actually resulted in a huge turning point for me, which is one of the reasons I include it in this book.

Being a giver has always been part of me and who I am deep inside, but it didn't always bring good things in my life. I was often told that I had a big heart and I gave too much. I gave to the detriment of myself a lot of the time. Maybe you have also seen this in your own life. My heart would go out to anyone who was down on their luck or needed someone and immediately I would be whatever they needed—friend, advisor, helper, giver of anything they needed. I gave and gave without boundaries.

I gave like a river without a dam until one situation taught me to build a dam. Now, I still provide but I give with a strategic and incredibly well-designed barrier.

It was around early 2006 when this story began. My brother was in prison, ironically enough. During a visit, he told me about this friend of his who was also in the same prison. He told me how this person didn't have anyone to come to visit him or write to him. He was going to be in there for a very long time. 'I know how much you love to help people', my brother said. 'Would you write to him and maybe come visit him once in a while'?

Me being me, I agreed. I jumped at the chance to help this lonely person whom my brother seemed to think was a charming person. So, we began writing, and I went to see him a couple of times. Before long we had struck up a friendship and I would go as far as saying I became very fond of this person. He began relying on me for everything he needed. His uncle, or at least that's what I was told, would put money in my bank account, and I would buy him what he needed. He would often ask me to keep some money for myself to use to cover my expenses of going to see him and getting his things. Everything was great as far as I was concerned. This was a sweet friendship, and I wasn't being taken for granted for once.

Soon, though, he began to be a bit more demanding. He wanted other people to put money in my bank account, claiming it was money he was owed. Small amounts at first and only a couple of payments here and there. Then the sums were getting bigger and from several different people. He even told me to keep a certain amount for myself if I needed any money as long as I kept the rest safe for him. I am a highly intelligent person, and I knew deep down something wasn't right. However, I was also a very giving person, maybe naively so, and I kept pushing down my suspicions and my discomfort because I wanted to help. To be honest, I was a single mum with three sons, and the extra money he was giving me was helping me a great deal. That factor helped turn down the volume on my discomfort.

Whenever I would get a little too uncomfortable and voice my concerns, he would always tell me how much he needed me and how he couldn't be without me. I was the only person he had, the only person he trusted, and he knew how to reel me back in again and again. People were now contacting me directly; girlfriends and friends of other inmates. My suspicions became too loud. I couldn't quiet them or ignore them any longer. I wasn't from that world. I didn't know for sure what was happening, but I was smart enough to know it wasn't legal and it wasn't right.

My smarts were finally taking over my penchant for giving without boundaries. I began refusing to let people put money in my account. He wasn't happy and his approach became pushy. I still refused. He wasn't nicey-nicey anymore; no more, *I need you, you're the only person I have and trust.* Now it was, *you better do this. I need that money. You are the one that I want to do this because I know you won't screw me over.*

Nothing was keeping the volume low on my suspicions, and my discomfort was at an all-time high. I was terrified of what I had gotten myself into, and no amount of money could convince me to stay involved. I now refused point-blank to accept any payment from anyone, to go see him again, or buy him anything he needed. Then came the threats, but nothing direct enough from him, of course. He would say, 'you will see what happens if you don't help me'.

These were indirect threats that I knew were serious, but would be difficult to prove. I reported it to the prison and stopped all communication. The prison blocked him from calling me or writing to me directly. I kept £600 of his money after I did that. I don't know what I was thinking, but I wasn't being smart. At the time I thought I was getting out and washing my hands of the whole situation. Then came the calls and texts from other people. Vague threats like, *I know where you live and where your children go to school.* There were lots. I reported it to the police. They took a statement and made copies of the texts. I thought nothing was direct enough to take any action. The police alerted the prison, and the prison moved him across the country. The threats didn't stop, though, and the police couldn't do anything. They said that unless there were explicit, provable threats or if something happened in person then they couldn't do anything.

I was so terrified by this point that I moved away without telling anyone where I was going. No forwarding address, not even my family. I packed everything in a van and I went. I took two of my sons with me. My youngest son was living with his grandparents at that time, and I had to leave him behind. I changed my phone number and also my name. Those are the lengths I went to, to get away.

The threats stopped, and life slowly got back to normal. But just when I thought I had put it all behind me, the threats suddenly started again. I didn't know how or who and I still couldn't prove a thing. They knew where I lived, and I was now in fear for my life and for my son's lives. I tried giving the money back, but they weren't interested in that. They said that wasn't enough. It didn't make up for all the money lost, and they felt I was responsible for it. They wanted me to get involved in getting money for them, but I refused. The tipping point came when I got a message telling me some unknown person knew where my youngest son lived, and if I wanted to see him again, I had to sort this out.

The penny dropped. I was travelling back up north every two weeks to see my son, and that's how they must have found me. I didn't feel the police could protect me. I had tried that several times. I felt I had no other option but to sort this out. I agreed to meet this person to get the details of what they wanted me to do. Terrified, I went to the place. I met with a sweet young guy, not what I was expecting at all, and I certainly wasn't what he was expecting. He gave me an envelope with a passport inside and some bank details. I was told that a loan had been approved in this woman's name and I was to sign the passport in that signature and go to a specific branch and collect £6000. Then I was to bring it back to him. There is a reason I say this person was a sweet young guy, and in some ways, I need to thank him, because he helped me to prevent more of this nightmare.

'If I do this will it be over'? I asked him.

He looked at me surprised, 'I should not tell you this, but you are so nice, and you really shouldn't be involved in this. You will not get out of this unless you get caught'.

I didn't quite understand. 'What you are saying is they are going to want me to do more'?

'They will keep making you do this until you get caught.. 'Once you get caught you won't be any use to them anymore. The best thing you can do is get caught'.

The idea of getting caught really messed with my mind. I didn't want to do it at all, and I certainly didn't want to get caught. I thought about all of my options.

'What if I go to the police with the evidence'? I asked him.

In a cautious voice he said, 'that wouldn't end well for you either. If you don't have a bad record you will get off with a slap on the wrist. That's your best bet and they won't bother you anymore'.

I couldn't see any other way out so I went for it. I made the only decision I felt I could make at the time to end this nightmare. I went to the bank, knowing I was going to get caught. I didn't even sign the passport. I walked up to the window, and as I gave the teller the passport I said, 'I want to withdraw a £6000 loan that has been deposited to that account'.

He looked at the passport, then looked at me for what felt like an eternity. He said convincingly, 'give me a moment while I go arrange the withdrawal'.

He was gone for a few minutes, meanwhile I was praying. On the one hand, he didn't come back with £6000, and on the other hand, I didn't get caught. I believe that's referred to as being "between a rock and a hard place."

Have you ever been in a similar situation where you felt you were damned if you did and damned if you didn't?

The teller came back. 'It's taking a while longer than expected to get the cash. Would you like to follow me and sit upstairs for a few minutes while they get it done'?

I followed him upstairs, and he took me into a plush area reserved for business clients. He got me some water and left me to wait. This was not happening the way I imagined it. I thought the police would have stormed the bank by now, grabbed me, and then dragged me out in front of everyone. I was so nervous; my head was spinning. It felt like I was going to have a heart attack. I started to think they were actually getting the money and this nightmare wasn't going to be over so easily. A sudden calm came over me. Somehow, I felt that they weren't getting the money, and it was going to be okay. It had dawned on me the police were coming, and it was really over. Just at that moment, I heard footsteps of more than one person coming up the stairs. It was the police. In a calm manner, one of the officers said, 'I want you to follow us outside. We don't want customers to pay attention or be alarmed. Are you willing to walk with us as if nothing is wrong'?

I agreed. I was so calm; I smiled and went with them. It felt like they knew I hadn't freely decided to attempt to commit this crime. They took me outside and put me in a police van.

As we were driving away, I was looking out of the window for the sweet guy because I knew he was outside waiting for me. I saw him on the corner. He just tipped his head as if to say *good for you*. I felt that I had actually done the right thing. Finally, I felt inside I had made the right decision. I also felt I had stood up for myself (you know that part is always important to me). I took back self. I took back my power. And I let self be my weapon.

I told the police everything. They charged me with attempted fraud. I had to go to court to prove my case, and I had all of the evidence I needed. The evidence from the police, the prison, the texts, and the letters. The judge took all of it into consideration and even commented on how he felt I had been let down by the system. He gave me a twelve month suspended sentence. Thankfully it was now over. Or perhaps not...

I never thought I would have this story to tell, and I certainly didn't set out to create it. I am not going to justify one bit of my actions in this situation, and I accept full responsibility for my part in it. But there is a lesson in this for all of us. I want you to understand that it is so easy for any of us to find ourselves in a situation we feel like we can't control. I want you to see how easy it is for someone to manipulate us and it has nothing to do with intelligence. Even the most highly intelligent people can be manipulated because the person doing the manipulating is parasitic. They attach themselves to us, and they prey on our weaknesses. They prey on our vulnerabilities and they use them to their advantage. They find us because we are givers with victim mentalities, and we are the perfect victims for narcissistic people. They need us to feed off of and to make them feel better about themselves.

Master yourself. Defy your self-inflicted suffering. We self-impose suffering when we assume we are not enough. Believe the universe would not have wanted you born if you weren't made for something great. Don't let anybody be the puppet master of your life. Cut the strings, take back your power, and take back self. Let self be your weapon. Smile and rise, smile and rise.

I don't know you yet, but I love you still.

Chapter 11
Going to Prison

Yes, I know, I fought, and I won the attempted fraud case. However, what happened next was almost a year later. I had been on a driving ban due to all of the stress from before. The ban was now over. I had neglected to get my licence renewed after the ban. One day driving along I got pulled over by the police. I had my son Michael in the car and as we were pulling over, I turned to Michael and said, 'I'm going to prison'.

'What are you talking about'? he asked.

'I don't know but I have a bad feeling I'm in serious trouble'.

It was now 2009, just days away from the suspended sentence being over for the attempted fraud. I was charged with driving while on a driving ban, and now driving without insurance because of the ban. I found myself going back to court and I was under no illusion this would go well. My lawyer had also warned me it would most likely be a custodial sentence. I was prepared. I made arrangements for my sons. I left bank cards and credit cards at home and all the details with my son Michael for my accounts.

The judge took exception to this mistake, which was now one of many. There was no sympathy for what I had previously gone through, and I wasn't looking for any either. He sentenced me to ten weeks in prison. With good behaviour, I would serve five weeks. I was in shock. No matter how much I prepared or expected it, I really couldn't. There was always hope that under the circumstances the universe would conspire in my favour again.

I didn't stop crying from the moment he gave his verdict. I cried the whole time I was in the holding cells downstairs, when they put me on the bus, and the entire time they were processing my arrival. I cried so much they were worried I was going to hurt myself. I must have cried for almost five days on and off. I was on what they call the induction wing, which is meant for new prisoners until they place you on a proper wing. That was the only wing where you could be in a cell on your own. I only came out of the cell to get my food and went straight back in. I didn't talk to anyone. I didn't want to know anyone, and I didn't want them to know me either.

The person in charge of the induction wing was so lovely and very helpful. He kept stalling my move to a proper wing and kept me on the induction until he could find a cell somewhere he felt I could cope. Finally, time ran out, and he couldn't stall anymore. He had to move me. I was there for almost three weeks; the maximum was meant to be seven days. However, during my time there, I was able to spend time thinking about things. After the first five days of allowing myself to wallow and feel sorry for myself, I decided this wasn't going to beat me. I decided my mum hadn't put me on this Earth to waste one day, let alone five weeks. I took Self back again. So, I did the only thing I could at that time. I got every self-help book from the library and read them over and over. Every chance I got I went to the library to exchange books. There weren't a lot of choices, but I learned as much as I could. I took notes and scribbled away like crazy. I started to make a plan for my life. I began to focus on what I wanted from life and who I wanted to be. I began to think of the difference I could make in the world. I became determined that I wouldn't waste another day when I left there.

When I was moved onto a standard wing, I was moved onto a quiet side that had mostly enhanced non-violent people. I shared a cell with a woman who I became great friends with. I call her Z. She was there because she didn't have a visa for the UK and I helped her with her appeal, filling in all of the paperwork she had to complete and reading all of the paperwork they sent her. English wasn't her first language and she was struggling with everything. She also had terrible diabetes, and she wasn't coping very well. They put us together because they felt I would look after her, and she would be an excellent quiet person for me to be with. They were right. We inspired each other. We kept each other positive, and we share a beautiful friendship.

I learned what she had gone through in her own country; the terrible, unbelievable acts of violence, sexual abuse, and the death of some of her family members. She managed against all the odds to make it to the UK with her husband, and her son was born in the UK. I knew her story to be true because of the pain in her eyes when she entrusted me to hear her and believe her. I also read it in her paperwork. I understand now that I was there for her. This is where I really began stepping into myself and who I was meant to be. I started to understand how I wanted to show up in this world and first embarked upon the work I have become so passionate about now.

She inspired me. Her struggle and pain made me want to help as many people as possible. It's part of the reason I support women and girls and why I plan to launch my own foundation. I have always been passionate about the crisis that other women like Z face. My mum brought me up with some awareness. However, this was the first time in my life, I was not only facing a real survivor of such atrocities, I was sharing a room, food, a toilet and my life with her. She was sharing hers with me as well. I could not be prouder to have shared everything with her and to call her my friend. I came face to face with who I wanted to be. I met her son and her husband. We wrote to each other. I went back to visit her. Being a fellow inmate, I had to wait two months before I was allowed to see her. We kept in touch, and I saw her after she went home. She says it's because of me that she got to go back to her son and her husband. It's really because of her, but the universe brought me to support her and provide a little backup.

Due to a delay and a mistake with my paperwork being processed by probation I could not be released at five weeks. They gave me a choice. I could be released a week late with an ankle bracelet for another four weeks which would have taken me to the full ten weeks sentence, or I could choose to stay another three weeks and go home free. I could, of course, complain and make an appeal to get the paperwork corrected, but that wouldn't have done much good. I would have been gone by the time it ever got processed, let alone fixed. So, I opted to stay, and I ended up serving eight weeks, and two days in total. I came home August 10th 2009.

My time in prison wasn't easy. I was attacked and hit in the face. I had hot coffee thrown on me, and some people tried to intimidate me verbally. The funny thing is the more they did these things to me the more I stepped into myself. They didn't like that I didn't shy away or get scared, but I also didn't retaliate. They didn't know how to deal with me. I certainly wasn't meant to be there, and that's not what I say that's what some of the other inmates told me, for various reasons. Some didn't like me because I wasn't meant to be there, they didn't like my presence because I wasn't like them. One inmate that really didn't like me (although I suspect secretly she did and I would even go as far as saying she respected and admired me) told me that she felt my presence on the wing when I wasn't near her. She could hear my voice, and she could see how I carried myself, and she didn't like it. She said that I walked around as though I was better than them. She would go out of her way to speak to me and attempt to goad me, but these little battles of the mind always resulted in her getting angry and at herself mainly. We all know that I was a source for her insecurities to come flooding out and since everyone else was scared of her she gravitated to me like a moth to a flame for stimulation mainly I suspect. Some said I wasn't meant to be there because they liked me, and they also felt I had a presence that was positive, kind and loving, and that I wasn't meant for there. I want to tell you now, however, horrible the difficulties were, and there was a lot not mentioned. I choose to focus on the positive and the good that came out of that time. I quickly became the go-to person for advice, encouragement and care and I'm grateful for that. I'm thankful for the experiences in that building with the people I met that have helped shape who I am today.

Prison was the first time in my life I began to realise just how powerful my presence was, how I could inspire, advise, empower, encourage, and bring positivity to those who need it and challenge those who don't think they need it. I learned a lot about myself. I also discovered my limits were few and my strength infinite. I learned the universe is always conspiring in your favour and life happens for you, not to you. You just have to choose what you do with what life throws at you.

I joke, and I say I had an eight-week break to focus on myself and take time to see who I could become at Her Majesty's pleasure and it was for free. Nothing is ever free (it's just my sense of humour and how I choose to deal with things). I lost time with my sons because I was in prison. I lost my business because I was in jail. I lost my home because I was in prison. I had to fight to rebuild my life when I got home. I was so ready to fight the world when I came out of there. I had this absolute determination that those eight weeks were going to mean something. I was going to achieve everything I ever wanted, and I realised some pretty wild dreams. I also learned if you want everything in your wildest imagination, your imagination has to be pretty damn wild in the first place. I fought in court and got my equipment and furniture back from my business. I found an investor for my business one month after coming home. I found new premises, and I began to rebuild. I fought the people who thought they could destroy me with a story in the newspaper, so I gave the full story myself instead. I challenged those who called the centre manager where my business was now located because I told him everything in person. I lost so much in those eight weeks, and I had to fight the consequences for a long time after, but what I gained in the process can never be taken away.

I learned how to be me. I learned how to use my presence powerfully. I learned that being bold meant being vulnerable, and it also meant being fearless. Be all of you, through suffering, but recognise what you've gone through without being a victim to it. You must be the owner of your suffering. You must accept both the light and the dark. Without the dark, there is no light. And that actually gave me pride. I realised that very few people could turn around what I did. I was able to turn around every negative thing in my life and use it for power and for fuel. I realised I would always be okay if I just kept moving forward.

I knew deep down that my foundation was broken. I had to rebuild. I had to recreate myself to *Rebel Woman*—the woman that I wanted to be—not what the world or life made me. Life experience made me a scared, angry, insecure, needy girl. When you look at that mirror every day and you do not like the reflection staring back at you, and you choose to live in that, that is your fault. We have the ability to recreate ourselves, and I decided to do so in the form of *Rebel Woman*.

Rebel Woman is a person who decided she no longer wanted to be insecure, afraid, and broken. This Woman. chose to be her own hero, to be a woman that she could look up to.

When I look in the mirror, I want to see someone I'm proud of. The only way to do that is to take out that big rubbish bin that was in my life. I had to start emptying it. And Michelle Moffat couldn't do that. That's much too frightening. *Rebel Woman* had to go back there and say, 'I've got this. Let's go. Let's woman up'.

I've realised in life that you have to take Self back every day. It's not a case of taking her back once, and now you're fixed or triumphant. You have to take back Self every single day until no one can ever take it from you again. Until you have mastered yourself, this entire journey we are all on is about mastering ourselves. The universe is always conspiring in our favour, and I believe the universe was most definitely conspiring in my favour that day. When else or how else was I going to give myself eight weeks to work on myself, to step away from my life, my sons and my business for eight weeks to fully and totally focus on my life?

Recreate yourself, man or woman up, and take Self back. You know you can.

I don't know you yet, but I love you still.

Chapter 12
My Brother Slowly Killed Himself

Robert was my best friend growing up. We were always together having fun and doing silly things. We went everywhere together. I was a proper tomboy, always covered in mud and hanging around with all of my brother's friends.

After my mum passed away, just before my brother's eighteenth birthday, he was never the same person. He began taking drugs and getting into trouble. It was tough and we never really talked about her as a family. We didn't have any proper grieving.

My brother went down a path that he couldn't control and no matter how hard I tried, he didn't come back fully. There were times when he would do well, and it would seem like he finally found the turning point, but the wind would change and he would be lost again. It took him years of pain, suffering, and destroying himself. Years of addiction and going in and out of prison. Years of doing bad things to people he loved, and I was no exception. Over the years he stole from my home, assaulted me, and emptied my entire bank account, but I loved him still.

The last time I ever saw my brother alive was when he badly assaulted me. He had been staying with me because I was the only one who would take him in. When he first arrived at my place, I warned him that if he took anything from me again I would disown him and press charges. I watched him go through drug withdrawal on my sofa, and this was not the first time. Three days of watching him rolling around in excruciating pain telling me he was going to die, sweating, and breathing heavy. He was crying and screaming in pain, begging me to get him some drugs. It finally passed, and he was slowly getting better.

A few weeks passed, and he was starting to gain weight and look healthy. He seemed happier and was beginning to talk about his future. I began to hope that he had finally turned the corner and I had my little brother back.

However, I came home early one day, and he wasn't there. Immediately I knew something was off. I ran upstairs, opened my wardrobe, pulled all of the things out to get to my jewellery box which I had hidden, and everything was gone apart from my mum's ring and necklace.

I called my father and told him and asked him to come get my brother's things. If my father found my brother, he was not bring him back to my house. The police were looking for him, and if he came by I would alert the authorities. Later that night my father, his wife, and my brother came to my house. I was cooking dinner and they just let themselves in.

Michael was watching TV in the front room. Stephen was out somewhere (thank god, because he would have gotten involved), and Liam was with his grandparents.

I told them to get out. I had made myself clear earlier. An argument ensued, and I began to call the police. I walked away into the hallway. I locked the front door and put the key in my pocket. At this point, all three of them were screaming at me and trying to stop me from calling the police. All three of them at some point in this situation assaulted me. It lasted about fifteen minutes; screaming and shouting and fending off blows and trying to defend myself.

Then, at some point, there was a break in the noise, and we could hear Michael screaming in the front room terrified.

'Your grandson is out there screaming,' I shouted, 'while you all beat his mother up'. This made them stop. My brother ran upstairs and climbed out of an upstairs window, dropped down onto the roof of my car, smashed the back windscreen of my car with my son's hockey stick, and ran off.

When I came back downstairs, my father and his wife were sitting in my front room as if nothing had happened; as if they were there for a visit. The police arrived and arrested them both. They gave her a caution because she had admitted to hitting me and she didn't have a criminal record. They charged my father with grievous bodily harm. My brother was eventually caught after making lots of threats against me to drop the charges. But he was charged with grievous bodily harm, criminal damage, intimidating a witness, and threatening criminal damage.

My father and my brother both plead not guilty at the pre-trial hearing. People in my family and friends could not believe that I had my father and brother charged and went ahead with a court trial. I was raising three sons, and it was my responsibility to teach them they could not behave like that and no one, not even their own family, was allowed to treat them like that. My brother didn't turn up to court and while I was waiting in the witness room waiting for the trial to begin against my father the court clerk came and told me the trial had been cancelled. My father had now changed his plea to guilty and they didn't need me as a witness. My father received a twelve month suspended sentence. My brother went on the run and was never caught. I never saw him again, and I never spoke to him again. He would call whenever I was at my sister's and beg to talk to me, but I never spoke to him.

Nine years passed and I refused to speak to him each time. In that time, he had continued his addiction to drugs and alcohol. He got married to a woman who also had a problem with alcohol. I was at home one night in January 2011. I was pregnant with my daughter at that time. It was after 10 p.m. and my phone rang. It was my sister and I was annoyed that she was calling me so late.

She told me my brother was in the hospital in Glasgow and he was dying. My sister was always very dramatic, so I told her to stop being so emotional and explain. She said the nurse had told them he only had twenty four hours or less to live. I thought this was crazy and she was being over the top. I spoke with my uncle who had arrived at the hospital. 'He's in a critical way Michelle',, he said. 'If you want to see him before he goes, you better get here tonight'.

I lived at least five hours away from Glasgow at that time. We left immediately and went to pick my sister up on the way.

I drove as fast as I could but my uncle called when we were thirty minutes away to tell us we were too late. We got to the hospital, and I couldn't go in the room. I didn't know how to feel. So much had happened. I stood in the doorway, but I still couldn't go in. As we were leaving the hospital, I had the urge to go back alone to see him. I entered the room this time, but I couldn't go near him. He didn't look like himself; my brother. I stood by the bottom of the bed, and I said to him, 'you stupid, stupid boy. You had a whole life ahead of you. You wasted a perfectly good life, thirty-six years; wasted and you could have done so much in this world'.

I was busy giving him a right telling off, when a nurse walked in. 'It's okay', she said. 'You can go up to him. You can touch him'.

But I still couldn't. He was only thirty-six and died of liver cirrhosis. Can you imagine how much abuse he must have put himself through to kill himself like that? I picked his things up from the morgue. I then picked up his death certificate and I went to see his wife who I had never met before. She couldn't even understand what we were trying to tell her. She was bedridden and not very with it mentally; he was her carer apparently. The place they lived was run down, and the house was disgusting. My feet were sticking to the floor. When we left the house, I said to my uncle, 'he's better off where he is now'. Of course I didn't want him dead, but after seeing how his life was, I knew he was in a better place. And he was with his mum. His wife died exactly two weeks later of the same disease. My uncle and I planned his funeral and made all the arrangements.

I believe my brother never got over my mum's death. I believe he was lost and could just never find his way back. He wasn't an evil person. He wasn't a thug like everyone thought. The person lying in that coffin wasn't my brother; not the brother I knew or grew up with. My brother was a beautiful, kind, loving, warm, generous, and fun person who was always full of life and smiling. He would have done anything to help anyone. He was simply broken and didn't know how to fix himself. What I'm telling you, I wrote in his eulogy. I was the only person that spoke at his funeral.

It took a lot for me to write that eulogy and it took a lot to focus on the positives about my brother. I spent a long time wishing I had gotten there before he died. If I had, I could have told him I loved him. I could have been there for him at the end. That's been the hardest thing for me, even now. Despite wrestling with a lot of emotions, regrets, and guilt I managed to find the good and the love. I also managed to find peace in the fact I had done everything I ever could for him. I never turned my back on him. I always had love for him. I still had hope for him, and I always wanted the best for him—he always knew that.

I was always there for my brother when it mattered the most. But I had to protect my family and live my life my way with my choices.

Make the choices that serve your life. Don't let anyone change or influence what you need to do for you or your family. I took a lot of criticism for the choices I made after those events. I did what I had to do for my life. That didn't mean I stopped loving him or I stopped wanting the best for him. It also didn't mean that I ever stopped hoping for a better outcome. I always imagined one day he would finally clean his act up, and we would be best friends again. I never imagined that I would have to find that friendship in my heart instead of real life. He made his choices, and I made my choices. You make your choices.

I don't know you yet, but I love you still.

Chapter 13
My Marriage Breakdown

I left my daughter's dad. In fact, I was the one who had left all of my relationships. Each time I was determined not to stay in an unhappy relationship. With this man there was no love and the relationship was not great. We (I) tried to fix it for a long time, longer than I should have but I couldn't.

The focus I choose regarding my ex-husband is not about blame. It's not about who was wrong or right; it's not about the bad but rather the good. The good in the sense that we had a relationship and we were in love once. More so, we have a beautiful daughter who we always gave the best of ourselves to.

I walked away because I wanted more from a relationship and more from life. I wanted my daughter to have more and to know that she came from a loving relationship. I wanted her to know what a loving relationship was. To understand how to be in a loving relationship. I wanted her to know she was loveable and worth nothing less than the most amazing, loving relationship.

I've never had the kind of relationship I have always truly wanted, but I won't ever settle for less. Being madly in love, excited to be with each other, proud of each other, a great connection, and a deep bond. Enjoying the heck out of life with each other and building an amazing, loving relationship together. I want to have a deep connection and a real partnership in every way with my person. I only desire to build a life and a relationship with my best friend. Something beyond ordinary, built on trust and friendship. We'd be building a dream. We would support each other and push each other to achieve more. We would love deeply and cherish each other. We'd have the kind of relationship that makes the world jealous when they see us together. I want my daughter to grow up in that kind of relationship; to model her own relationship on that framework.

This would be, and is, a wonderful gift to give my daughter. It's the kind of beautiful gift we should all give ourselves and our children. That is the kind of relationship we should all have for ourselves and the standard we should have for our lives. Some have said my standard is too high. Some have said I want too much; it isn't realistic or obtainable. I wholeheartedly disagree. You are the creator of your life, and you are the only person who sets your standards and gets to choose what you want. Don't ever settle; passionately protest mediocrity. You deserve what you want. Set your standards high. If they aren't high, you can't fly.

I'm not suggesting you go off and leave your partner because it isn't exciting or that you should go off chasing some fairytale. But you should have the kind of relationship you want and if you aren't currently getting that then you have to first get clear on what you want. Then you have to change what you have by working at it or by leaving. Have the courage to give yourself the beautiful gift of everything you have ever dreamed of in your life and your relationship. You won't regret it.

My daughter's dad isn't a horrible person. He's just not my person. He didn't want to put the work in. He didn't want to fly high. He was happy enough with the way it was, and I wasn't.

I have to fly. I have to have something vibrating higher. I have to have my person. I have to have my standard. Set your standards high and don't ever let anyone convince you they are too high. Have the courage and the conviction to go after what you truly want; don't ever settle.

Fly, fly, fly.

I don't know you yet, but I love you still.

Chapter 14
Journey to the new me

The journey to the new me began in 2009 when I was in prison. The change happened when I began to focus on myself and do the inner work. It also had a lot to do with the experience I had there and the people I met, particularly Z. I was always interested in personal development before. I had read books and gone to seminars. However, now, I couldn't get enough. I wanted to learn everything I could, and I seriously wanted to work on myself. My mind was so open to everything, and I was enjoying it. This journey of self-improvement is one I will always be on. I do at least one hour of personal development every day. That may be listening to an audiobook, a meditation, visualisation, or working on a transformational course such as Life Book. These are just some examples. It really depends on what my goal or focus is at any given time.

Although the journey developed there, it took on a whole different direction after I came home. I was hell-bent on changing everything. I knew I was going to have to fight to rebuild my life. I decided I was going to face everything head-on, and I was finally going to step into me fully. I began coursework on healing grief, anger, abuse, love, your inner child, and more. If it had 'healing' in the title I most likely took part in it. I also participated in a whole bunch of courses and seminars on stepping into your true potential. I followed that up with anything that related to creating the life you want and transforming yourself.

My journey took its biggest twist after my daughter was born. I not only gave birth to her, but I gave birth to a new me. This is when I began to be the real me; the me I always wanted to be and the one I knew deep down I've always been. She had just gotten lost somewhere under all of the stress, anger, and grief. I felt complete now. I felt life had given me a second chance. I knew I was going to be the mother I had always so desperately tried to be, but I was going to do it differently. I had learned from my wounds. I was going to teach this little girl to be the woman I always wanted to be and even more. I was going to give her so much love, she would never have to question what love was. That is one thing I knew I could do. Despite the mistakes I made with my boys I always gave love.

I had a complicated pregnancy from the beginning with my daughter. My pelvis actually collapsed too. I was in constant and sometimes excruciating pain. I couldn't walk properly. I couldn't sit or get up from a chair on my own and I also couldn't go to the bathroom on my own. It took almost one year after she was born for me to begin to really take control of the situation and set up my business again. I had around ten months of physiotherapy to help recover, and I was told not to go back to running my salon and being a massage therapist. I couldn't accept that. I couldn't imagine a world where I didn't see my clients and do massages. My physiotherapist could either help me to deal with it or not. The first three vertebrae of my spine were being crushed due to the angle of my pelvis, and standing doing massage all day was not going to make that better. My physiotherapist taught me some stretches that I could use throughout the day and stand in a half squat all the time. For six months, I was in pain all day long. I started my day doubled over and ended it the same way. Eventually, the pain began to grow less severe. I was determined not only to rebuild my business again but to be an active woman and mum.

Before my pregnancy, I used to work out hard. I had a personal trainer three times per week. I went to the gym four to five times a week, and I went for a run around the lake most lunchtimes. That had become my way of dealing with stress.

After my pregnancy and my recovery from my pelvis collapsing, I had gained a lot of weight. Weight loss was my next path on the journey to the new me. To help with this, I realised I needed to let go of a lot of emotional baggage I had carried which was holding me back physically and mentally.

I just had one final road to navigate, and that was to reveal all of me underneath by shedding the emotional padding and protection I had been carrying through various parts of my adulthood. I had weight challenges throughout my adulthood, like many people do. I would lose weight and then gain more back; it was an up and down process. This time I knew what the problem was, and I could fix it with the right solution. I realised that at times in my life, and this period being no exception, I would eat my pain and emotions. This time I was experiencing both physical and emotional pain, as well as not feeling loved in my marriage. It required a lot more stuffing back down and therefore, a lot more eating. Before I left my husband, I already knew I had to process my emotions and I needed to work on me more.

That's when the most in-depth part of my journey started. I made the decision to not just shed the weight, but to shed every single bit of my past and truly take back Self. I learned to love myself and put myself first. I left my husband. I let go of one hundred and forty-nine lbs. My business was now thriving, and so was I. I now loved myself deeply. I launched my skincare brand. I became a high-impact coach. I found my purpose. I set up my brand and began my mission. No more eating pain or carrying around my past. No more emotional baggage, guilt, and anger. I have learned to live in the present moment and focus so much more on pure joy and love every day. I am a desire seeker and an adventure lover. I am creating my life the way I have always wanted to. I am on my way to becoming my best self every moment of every day.

You too can find this kind of fulfilment, but only by doing the inner work. I say this many times in this book, and I'll say it again—take back Self. He or she is extraordinary when you set that person free.

I don't know you yet, but I love you still.

Chapter 15
Claims of Sexual Abuse

January 2016 while on a visit to Paris and Versailles I received a call from my oldest son Stephen. It's a phone call I will never forget. He sounded flustered and concerned. He told me that my sister had been to see him and had said some awful things about me. I laughed and told him not to worry. 'But mum, you don't understand', he said, unwavering in his concern. 'The things she has said are horrible'.

I laughed again. 'Don't worry, she's always saying terrible things about me'.

'No,' he said. 'This time it's very different, and I don't know how to tell you'.

'Okay,' I said, his concern finally registering with me. 'Now you are worrying me. What is it'?

He began to stutter and stammer, unable to get the words out. I was getting frustrated, and after more stuttering and me coaxing him to speak, he finally blurted it out. 'Aunt Rose has accused you of sexually abusing her since she was little and that you did it all her life'.

'Excuse me'? I said. 'What did you just say'?

'I know mum. I don't know how else to tell you. I shouldn't have to say such a thing. She came to see me and spent about two hours telling me all of these details. She then asked me if you had ever sexually abused me; if you had ever touched me anywhere. I told her no. I don't know how she could have asked me something like that'.

I was in shock and incredibly angry. Up to that point, I had been through a lot with my sister. She had her issues, and I had always supported and helped her. This was another level of hurt and defamation even for her. I couldn't stop thinking about this vile accusation. I couldn't understand it. What was her motivation? Why was she saying these things about me? I had a long time to think about it before I could actually do anything about it; before I could see her face to face and try to make sense of it. I was travelling but I decided I was going to go see her when I got back in the country. I wanted to see her face to face and hear her accusations and explanations for myself. I didn't live close to her, so it took a few days to make this possible.

To give you some perspective, I am five years older than my sister. The way she was describing this accusation to my son sounded like she was around two years old and I was seven when this alleged abuse began. She was basically describing me as a monster—a sexual predator. A vile, disgusting, and depraved human being. The pain at being accused of this was unbearable.

What hurt even more was this girl lived with me after our mum died. She also lived with me as an adult, of her own free will. In fact, she didn't make a choice to live with me once in her adulthood, she lived under my roof during several periods. She even asked to be placed with me by probation when she was released from prison. I was present in her life throughout. I visited her regularly in prison. I sent her money. I took care of her through every high and every low. I was always her first call when she needed anything, especially money. I was there during labour when her firstborn, my niece, was born. My niece would stay with me, and I would take her out on weekends alone. In fact, I was present in all of her five children's lives until they were taken by social services, due to her personal issues. I was part of all of the proceedings with social services and the court process. I travelled up and down the country every two weeks for meetings and court appearances. I am godmother to all five of her children. I always supported her, and I always tried my very best to be a positive, encouraging, loving force in her life. I gave her a job and wanted to teach her to want more from life (she told me she had lowered herself to work for me). And for reasons only she can explain, no matter how hard I tried she resented me more. It felt like the more I tried, the more she disliked me or hated me. I couldn't have been there more for this girl.

When I finally got back in the country, it was my youngest son Liam's birthday, so I took him for lunch. He also came with me to see my sister so that I would have a witness (little did I know how much I was actually going to need a witness). I thought I was just being smart and protecting myself from any further accusations. However, no one could have predicted what was about to come next.

The moment I knocked on her front door, she immediately began shouting through the window that she didn't want to talk to me. She screamed that if I didn't get away from her door, she was going to smash my face in and smash my car up.

'That's fine', I shouted back. 'But I'm going nowhere until you explain why you are accusing me of sexually abusing you since you were little'.

'Oh, you want the neighbours to hear'? she shouted, raising her voice ever more.

Yes, in fact, I did want the neighbours to hear. I wanted everyone to hear, I had nothing to fear and nothing to hide.

She came outside, and started screaming at the top of her lungs again about how she was going to smash my face in and smash my car up if I didn't go away.

'Please do', I said. 'If you feel that is what you need to do. I am going to do what I need to do. I want to know why you are accusing me of sexually abusing you. Why now out of the blue at the age of thirty-six'.

'You did sexually abuse me since I was little', she screamed. 'You touched me, and you made me touch you, and you have done it my whole life'.

'Explain the details', I demanded. 'Explain why you didn't cut me out of your life the moment you were old enough. Why was I allowed anywhere near your kids let alone be their godmother'?

She just kept repeating the same accusations and screaming that she was going to destroy my life and my business. 'You think you are so amazing with your life and your business. You think you're so smart; I'm going to destroy it all'.

The neighbours were now out in the street because of the noise. My son and I had gone to the other side of the road at this point. She then began shouting across the street to my son, 'I'm so sorry you have to find out like this. That you have to find out what kind of a person your mother is'.

'You're a liar', he shouted back defiantly.

She then started shouting at him. That was the point I had enough. My anger came raging out, not for me and the vile accusations against me, but for my son. 'You apologise to him', I yelled back. 'You are disgusting'.

She then began to cross the road shouting that she was going to smash my face in. I began to cross as well and she lunged at me, pushing me to the ground. She then spit in my face and shouted, 'That's what I think of you'.

I picked myself up and called the police. I reported that she had assaulted me and asked for them to attend immediately. My son and I continued to stand on the other side of the road while I waited for the police to arrive. While we were standing there, she was shouting, telling the neighbours her accusations and telling me that she had told My Sisters Place all about what I had done, and they were going to prosecute me. She said they believed her and that my father knew all about it and believed her too.

I didn't know what My Sisters Place was, but I later found out it was a refuge for abused women. Soon, the police arrived, and one officer spoke to me while the other officer took her inside her house. I told the officer what had happened and agreed to go ahead with official action against her. However, I also asked him if he could arrest me so that he could investigate these accusations she was making. He said he couldn't just arrest me or take me for questioning. The officer said that he would have to take a statement from her. He would investigate it, and if there were any case against me then he would arrest me. I had no choice but to agree. At that point I wanted to prove my innocence and stop this whole surreal experience.

He then left me outside and went into her house. He came back a short while later and told me that although she had explained her allegations to him in detail and claimed they were true, she was not prepared to make a formal complaint. She refused to give a statement because I'm her sister. I asked him what I could do about it. He said I couldn't do anything unless she made a formal complaint.

I could not believe what he was saying. 'Surely you can take my statement and conduct an investigation'? I asked. 'I will come with you now'.

'Without the victim making it official my hands are tied', he said. I couldn't believe he referred to her as a victim, Inadvertently or not.

I told him about her claim that My Sisters Place was going to take me to court and prosecute me.

'I can't see how that would be possible', he said incredulously. 'Any action would only be possible after an official complaint and an investigation that proved there was a case to answer'.

'So, she is just free to run around making accusations of this kind and there is nothing I can do to prove I'm innocent to protect my reputation'?

'You can take an injunction against her if she persists, or you could take a civil suit against her'.

He advised me to report any harassment or continued accusations to the police. Unfortunately, I have had to do just that, and she has received a warning for it. There was nothing else he could do, and I was left feeling helpless.

The police officers arrested her for the assault and took her away in the police car. I was given instructions to attend the police station later that day with my son to provide statements, which we did. She was charged with assault and released later that day. I hoped that while she was in the police station being interviewed, she would make the accusations official. I was told when I made my statement that she had claimed her accusations were valid during the interview but did not want to make it official.

Meanwhile, during a visit to my father's house that day, I discovered she had told him the same accusations two weeks earlier. He had told her she was being stupid and asked why this didn't come out earlier and why she hadn't told him or anyone else.

'Why didn't you inform me of this'? I asked him.

'I decided to ignore it because I thought it would blow over', he said nonchalantly.

He should have informed me despite how he felt about it. After getting nowhere with him, I contacted My Sisters Place. There was quite a bit of back and forth before they finally agreed to discuss the situation with me. They initially claimed they could not talk with me about my sister because of data protection. I didn't need them to discuss my sister— I needed to discuss my own situation. I was a victim of assault and abuse at the hands of my sister, and yet I was told I was the one being prosecuted. I had the right to know if this was true, and by law they had to discuss this with me.

Eventually, we discussed the accusations and the situation from my point of view. I was told that while my sister had discussed some details regarding me, that they were not in a position to prosecute me and they had advised police involvement which she refused.

I later found out that a friend of my sister had been given a new house to live in, in a beautiful area by My Sisters Place. They had also provided new furniture for the home. I have never confirmed this to be accurate, however, this information makes me believe that my sister made up this whole story in an attempt to also be moved by My Sisters Place and receive everything that her friend had been given. I was told that she never received any assistance from My Sisters Place because she did not move forward with an official complaint against me. I believe that she took these lies so far that she had to see it through. What I don't understand is why she continues to maintain these lies years later and has continued to cause friction in my family with accusations she refuses to back up.

The police told me if she continued to make accusations without officially reporting it they would arrest her for harassment. They also advised me to continue to report any incidents because they would then be able to take action against her. I have never allowed her in my life since that day in January 2016, and I never will. However, I have been told that she comments on my success and how proud she is that I'm her sister and that she thinks I'm going to have my own TV show like Oprah one day (which I am, of course).

No matter how much I have worked on this inside and no matter how much I have unpacked it and put it back together, it will never make sense. It is just something I accept as part of my story now. I have to adjust to it. But I will never run away and hide from it. As an actual victim of sexual abuse, these accusations have hurt me deeply. More importantly, she has made a mockery of pain and suffering that actual victims of sexual abuse go through when they report these incidents. She has belittled the courage they have to summon to get through the legal process of proving themselves and having people believe them. She's making it easier for people to ignore survivors when they have the courage to come forward.

In my experience, survivors of sexual abuse don't usually by choice stay around their abuser by choice. The survivor doesn't allow that abuser to be around their kids. They don't often wait after thirty years to blurt out their accusations over a cup of tea. They don't usually go to a women's refuge unless they are ready to face it or they need to get away from it. They don't often go running around the streets shouting about it to all the neighbours. They don't usually tell their children about it unless they have to. They most certainly don't often say it to their nephews nor do they wait for the abuser to call the police and then inform the police it's accurate but then refuse to make an official statement. They don't usually brag and broadcast how proud they are of the fruitful life the abuser has. I certainly wouldn't, and I've never worked with a sexual abuse victim who has taken this course of action (non-action).

Here are some facts about what actual victims of sexual abuse go through. I am a survivor and I work with a lot of survivors as well.

One in four women will be abused in their lifetime, and 90% of those women don't report it. Half of them suffer in silence never telling anyone, because it involves a family member or someone they know. The other half don't speak up because they fear not being believed. They are right because we don't believe them. But why? It's because he or she tells us disturbing and shocking things that we don't want to imagine or expect to hear.

We expect to hear a story of a half-dressed lower-class woman and a depraved man. We try to visualise what happened, but the visual is two dimensional. It's dark and it only lasts twenty seconds. There's no sound and no movement; as if no one was involved. When a woman tells her story of sexual abuse, it lasts longer than twenty seconds. We hear things we can't understand or accept and then doubts, suspicions, and questions pour in. This makes us feel bad so we protect ourselves from the discomfort.

There are two ways in which we typically protect ourselves from discomfort. For one, we turn the volume up on the parts of the story we expect to hear and the volume down on the parts we don't expect to hear. We do this so we can believe her, so we can feel confident she is really a victim. However, this in itself is victimisation of the victim. It is victimisation because to believe she's innocent we need to think of her as paralysed, helpless, and mute.

Or we do the exact opposite. We turn the volume up on the things we don't expect to hear, the things we don't want to hear, and we turn the volume down on the things we expect to hear. We do this so we can hold onto doubts and feel more comfortable about them. Questions come up that aren't really questions; they are judgements. Judgements that end with your verdict which is, *she asked for it.*

I have spoken out about my own taboo and painful topics in graphic detail as you know from reading this book and I believe this is the spark for change in our own healing and for society. It forms part of the very reason I do the work I do and the purpose I have in my life, which is to make a difference in people's lives one beautiful person at a time.

We are forced to make difficult choices to survive sexual assault. Let's encourage all women and men to call out unacceptable behaviour and be leaders of change. Let's turn up the volume on all of it and prevent it from existing. Sexual abuse is often called a woman's issue, intrinsically a man's problem tied to definitions of manhood. This isn't just a woman's or a man's problem. It is a human issue, and we start to make the change we need by turning up the volume and speaking out, making the graphic details so loud that no-one will be able to ignore it again. By making it undeniably present, and making it acceptable to speak the taboo. By taking away the silence, the taboo, and the blame. We can change the likelihood of it happening and be the change we all need to see.

Speak out, be loud, be the change.

I don't know you yet, but I love you still.

Chapter 16
The Friendship I Paid For Dearly

I had a friendship with a woman named Dorris that lasted almost a decade and not one I ever thought would end, however, it did. It was, as far as I believed, as close and as deep as any friendship could be. A sisterhood and part of my divine family as I would say. She's the type of person I never expected to hurt me to my core.

Dorris was a friend I put above myself in many ways. Our friendship had always been long distance. We met through an online networking group when I lived in Milton Keynes, and she lived in Somerset. We hit it off immediately; it was like finding a missing piece of myself. We would talk for hours and hours. I held Dorris in such high regard. I thought she was better than me, more successful than me, more focused than me.

Dorris witnessed the birth of my daughter. I invited her to every special occasion, celebration, business event, and everything in between. She was a bridesmaid at my wedding in Barbados, and godmother to my daughter. We had a friendship I thought was ride or die. I loaned her money so she could grow her business while I would put my plans on hold. I loaned her money to publish her book, which became a number one bestseller on Amazon. I even paid for a writing course we both took. I would loan her cash from my bank account and then have to put things I needed on credit cards. I did everything for her, things I didn't even do for myself. I would pay for trips, treats, dinners, and wine. When she visited me, I would give her free products and treatments from my spa. Every year in early January, we would go away for a couple of days and plan our year around what we wanted from our personal lives and our businesses. Of course, I paid for those trips.

In early 2017 after some serious encouragement from Dorris, I moved closer to her and into a house in Wiltshire. I was on my own where I had been living previously but she felt I had more of a network and support closer to her so I took the leap and made the move.

Dorris and I decided we were going to set up a business together, one that I had conceived some years earlier. We had been talking about setting it up for about three years at that point. I poured everything I had into the move and our new business. We visited a health conference in Las Vegas August 2017 together. And I had provided her with a few loans. Dorris did not invest anything financially. After returning from Las Vegas, I didn't see her or hear from her much for almost a month. She kept putting things on hold to concentrate on her projects.

Meanwhile, I was now beginning to run into financial issues, and she kept putting things on hold. Things got so bad for me financially that I was having problems with my rent and my landlord began eviction proceedings against me. Happily, I managed to resolve this. However, she still sat back without paying any of her debt or starting the business I'd paid to set up.

I was in dire financial straits for a variety of reasons and Dorris knew this. I didn't have enough money to get a minimum tank order of oil to heat my home. Dorris didn't even offer to get some of the money she owed me for me to heat my house for the winter. Dorris would come to visit and of course, eat the food and drink the wine I bought. Then she would comment on how it was so cold you could see your breath in the kitchen.

My daughter and I spent the entire winter with no central heating, living with fan heaters in the front room and one bedroom just to stay warm. To add to all of my financial issues, I spent the whole of Christmas and New Year alone in my freezing house. I didn't see Dorris once. So much for all of the encouragement to move promising me support from her, her mum and sister and several others. I ended up feeling more alone than I had ever felt. I was at the lowest I had been for many years.

In January 2018, I began to question myself. Why would I allow anyone to treat me this way? I started wondering why I would put myself through such hardship for someone who would certainly not do the same for me. She knew I was alone in a freezing house and she didn't even invite me to hers for one hour. I kept asking myself why I didn't put myself ahead of her and why I had been more than happy in the past to put myself aside for her.

I asked Dorris these same questions but she didn't give me much of a response. I decided that enough was enough. I was going to focus on myself and put myself first. I decided that I was never going to put anything I wanted on hold again. I was going to move forward into 2018 focused only on what I wanted. The beginning of every year is always about letting go of what isn't working.

I'm actually thankful that the last four months of 2017 were so severe and miserable. I realised I needed to be alone. I needed to feel so isolated that I became comfortable being alone. The only person I could concentrate on was me. That is the lesson the universe needed and wanted me to learn. I needed to be so alone because little did I know I was about to be entirely alone and have my heartbroken over someone I thought was a great friend. However, it turned out to be one of the best things that could have ever happened to me. Something happened inside me during that period of living in the cold and feeling alone—a combination of two things I dislike the most.

I realised I needed to love myself more. I didn't have enough love for myself. I had gone back to old habits, just like I did after all of those failed relationships. All those people I gave and gave and gave to. The unhealthy and unhelpful thought process that if I gave more, became more tolerant and loving and understanding; if only I did more, then everything would be okay and I would get back what I deserved from that person.

Life doesn't work like that; not when you are in that cycle. Life has givers and takers. Givers will give and takers will take. We are all broken in some way. The only choice we have to make is whether we want to stay broken or if we want to heal ourselves. The best thing that can ever happen to you is when you hit so low and you feel so alone that you can only think about how you are going to take care of yourself and heal.

I've always had my fighting spirit with me. She never leaves me and lets me learn the hard way sometimes. But she always comes out fighting. So, I decided to move forward with that business, and I removed Dorris from the company directorship, and she wasn't exactly bothered about it. I began to ask Dorris for my money, but she told me she couldn't pay me anything. Instead of playing nice as usual, I told her she needed to start paying me a monthly minimum. Self-love and putting self first was now incredibly important to me and it still is.

My original agreement with Dorris was that as long as I didn't need the money I was happy to wait for her to repay me. However, if I ever found myself in the position where I needed it, she would get it for me somehow. I reminded her of this, and she proceeded to tell me again she couldn't pay me anything, not even the £300 per month that I had asked her to commit to. I was livid. I could not accept the sheer audacity when Dorris proceeded to say to me that she would have to wait until she was more comfortable before she could pay me (which by her estimate was four or five months).

This set a fire inside me, not just because of what she said, but because I now knew I was going to put myself first no matter what. I told her that I would not accept her inability to pay me back. She would have to begin making payments because I had priorities, and they could not wait. I would not accept the way she was treating me. I began to take on the mindset, *how dare she treat me in such a way and how dare I ever accept anything that wasn't serving me again.* I insisted she pay and guess what happened next? She dropped my ass as fast and as heartlessly as you can possibly imagine.

All of our communication about repayment up to that point had happened via email. Not once did she come to see me or speak to me in person. Then I found myself blocked from not only her on Facebook but a group we were both in as well. I realised I wasn't getting the notifications, so I emailed her and she told me she felt it was best that she removed me. What a punch in the gut. Bearing in mind, we hadn't had a discussion let alone a heated argument.

Then, as if this whole situation couldn't get more hurtful, I saw her at a networking group that we both attended monthly and where everyone knew we were business partners and friends. Despite the issues, I wasn't going to treat her any differently than my friend. I went over to say hello, and I leaned over to hug her. She barely and half-heartedly lifted one arm and immediately turned and continued the conversation she was having. She ignored me the remainder of the night and my daughter, who was six at that time. My daughter asked me the next morning why Auntie Dorris didn't speak to us, and I just made an excuse that she was just busy. We never talked about Auntie Dorris again, and my daughter doesn't ask about her.

We never did speak in person again, not because I wasn't open to it. Although she happily tore me apart in emails telling me I had clearly never valued the time or advice she had given me or the few times she was physically there and present for me. I knew the value of all of that. I live in gratitude always and am thankful for the tiniest thing anyone does for me.

I was blindsided by what happened in this situation, and I beat myself up severely and repeatedly for not seeing it coming. How could a highly intelligent, strong, suffer-no-fools woman let this happen? How could I not see it coming and from the person that was closest in my world? I trusted her implicitly. But I was never enough, never important enough, and it felt like I was dropped in the trash like a piece of paper that was no longer useful. I was so hurt, I stayed alone practically wholly shut off from everyone for another eight months just working and taking care of my daughter. I didn't want anyone close to me again. I felt betrayed and used, but the truth is I was a willing participant and I take full responsibility for all of the pain and everything I gave to that friendship. I know now I haven't lost anything I wasn't meant to lose; it too shall pass. I was meant to go through that because I was meant to learn to be really alone because when you have been truly isolated and you have become so comfortable with being alone, you can cultivate your inner strength, inner peace, and connect with self-love in a way that you never imagined possible. Something magical happened in those twelve months—my rebirth, a complete transformation. Like a butterfly coming out of its cocoon, I needed to come out of mine. I wanted so badly to get back to my life fully, and I knew that the only way I could do this was to completely unpack everything and transform every relationship or situation in my life that simply wasn't working for me. So, I set out on a journey that would transform everything in my life as I knew it then and it has transformed me in ways I could never imagine.

Now, what I want you to do is to look at what relationships are not serving you and what needs to change in order for you to really connect with you and what you deserve. Figure out what kind of metamorphism you need for you to live the life you are genuinely in love with. What decisions do you need to make that ensure your love for yourself is the strongest and keeps you first?

Through the deepest betrayal I found the deepest love I could ever imagine for myself! I hope you don't have to go through betrayal before you tap into the most profound love and respect for yourself. When you have that level of love for yourself, you will only attract people with the capacity to love on the same level. No one will ever hurt you so deeply again.

I don't know you yet, but I love you still. (Love yourself more than anyone else can.)

Chapter 17
My Children

My heart, my soul and my greatest loves

I want to invite you to share in the most important and treasured relationships of my entire existence. If it wasn't for these four beautiful people I wouldn't have made it this far. Four different characters, souls, and influences on who I am today and how I show up in this world. Being a mother is the greatest reward and challenge of my life and it has certainly filled my life with joy, heartbreak, and love.

Stephen

With my firstborn, Stephen I never thought I could feel such love. It's not the kind of love that builds, it's a love that hits you all at once like a steam train running right over the top of you. It's the best feeling in the world and the scariest. He was perfect with piercing blue eyes that peered right through my soul. I just wanted to love him, hold him forever, and never let him go. I couldn't believe I had produced such a perfect and healthy human being. My life changed forever that day in so many beautiful and challenging ways. Although I could never have known the reality of the responsibility ahead of me, I wouldn't have changed it for the world. I had my little man I could love unconditionally and that is an extraordinary gift.

He was a good baby; he never really cried and slept right through the night most of the time from. He slept so much I used to nudge him to make sure he was still alive and check that he was breathing. Sometimes I would just sit and watch him sleep. He was so beautiful, and all I wanted to do was love him and give him the world. I felt like the luckiest mum in the world. Stephen has always had a great character. He's utterly charming. He has a shy-like smile but with a total glint in his eyes. He has an endearing giggle when he gets embarrassed, and flushed. He's always full of life, smiling, and talking a lot and asks about everything. He is bold and loud (wonder where he gets that from). He loves life and he's incredibly intelligent.

He was spoiled; first son, first grandson on both sides, and first great-grandson too. A lot of firsts and a lot of people wanting to give him all the attention and love they could. But all I wanted was to have him to myself. The end of the day was the best time when it was just him and me, and I got to snuggle with him and talk to him. Those times were so precious.

He had a rough start; a rocky relationship with his father, his parents splitting up, and the tension in our house. He was a happy baby despite that because he was surrounded by love. At six months old, I really did have him almost all to myself. My mum was there every day, but at night and in the mornings, it was just him and me.

After my mum died, he came back with me full time, and I don't think either of us coped with it very well for a while. But we found our way eventually. He was too young to understand why my mum wasn't there anymore, but I know it affected him still and he missed her.

He could be challenging to handle at times, but deep down, he is such a sweet soul. Very loving and caring, but he will do things his way just like me. We have always had the kind of relationship that was very good one minute and then the next we would be in battle. I loved him regardless, and despite the battles he always told me he loved me when all was said and done. His friends were at our house a lot, I was the cool mum as far as they were concerned, although he always protested about that.

He is a fantastic person with so much to offer the world. The best thing about having him so young is that now we are like friends. I was still growing up while he was growing up. I didn't always get it right, but it wasn't without trying and having his best interests at heart. He tells me everything at times, sometimes too much, and we have a great connection when we do get along. We are very alike—stubborn, vocal, passionate, sensitive, and immensely loving. It makes for a great relationship and an explosive one in equal measure, but it all comes back to love.

I'm excited about the future. I'm looking forward to seeing what he achieves and how he grows as a man. He isn't a dad yet, but I hope he becomes one because he would be great at it. I am so proud of him, and I love him just as much now as I always have. He has brought me so much joy and a little bit of heartache. But he will always be my baby boy, my firstborn, my first real true love. His eyes will always have my soul.

Michael

My second baby boy, Michael, was named after me. As soon as I had him there was a rush of love all over again. As a mother the capacity we have for love simply amazes me. He was beautiful, of course, as I knew he would be after having my first beautiful son. He was like a chubby little sumo wrestler weighing in at 10 lbs. and 4 ounces.

Michael was a good baby, although he didn't sleep as much as Stephen and he definitely loved his food. I never had to wake him up for a feed, that's for sure. He was calm and content, and he still is now. He has a mild nature and is loving and quiet; the complete opposite of Stephen. Michael is an efficient thinker, and he loves to learn everything he can. Our relationship was always close. He was definitely a mummy's boy. Michael liked to please and follow the rules, something that didn't go down well with Stephen; he called him the golden boy. There's no golden boy for me though, they are just very different people, and I love them equally but in different ways. Michael was less confident growing up. He didn't go out much. He liked to be at home. He is laid back, accepting, and goes with the flow. But rub him the wrong way, and he will let you know your place (wonder where he gets that from) directly but quietly and calmly. When he was a boy, he would talk to me about everything in his life, and we would talk for hours sometimes. He was always full of ideas. He is highly intelligent and very focused, sometimes quite single-mindedly. He is kind and gentle, and he has a big broad smile, although he liked to look moody most of the time. He has such a calm, soothing voice. He used to work on my reception in my salon and customers always praised how professional he sounded and could never believe he was my seventeen-year-old son. He had a much more serious attitude and a responsible approach to everything. He never got in trouble and always got good grades. He was like the dream child I never had to worry about and in a lot of ways blended into the background.

Michael left home at eighteen under not so amicable circumstances which was a complete shock to me at the time. I would never have expected that, and we lost our relationship. I am still heartbroken about it. We speak now, but it is a long way from the relationship I would love to have. There is a big chunk of missed time that I can never get back, but I remain hopeful for the future. He is a dad, and I am beyond proud of him as a parent. I like to think he is the parent he is today because of the way I raised him. I always knew Michael would be an amazing dad, but how he steps up as a man blows me away. He is adamant that his daughter is his full responsibility and takes great care of her.

He has told me that he found it difficult at times, growing up around my dysfunctional family. And when he became a father, he made a choice that he never wanted my granddaughter to grow up around that influence and so he decided to keep her away from my family, including me. He said he kept her away from me just so my family could never be involved. I understand that it wasn't always the best situation to grow up in, and I agree that my granddaughter should not have that in her life. I would dearly love for Michael to understand I did my best with the situation I found myself in. I didn't know how affected Michael was by these things, but I knew he never liked the drama.

I just hope that Michael can find it in his heart to understand I did the best I could at the time, and I always had my son's best interests at heart. I never set out to choose that lifestyle, but I do take responsibility for how it affected him. I think the kind of person and father he is speaks volumes about who he is inside, but I also think it speaks volumes of the actual influence I was on his life, the kind of mother I am, and the kind of grandmother I could be. I've always taught my children to aim high and achieve. I've always encouraged all of them to dream and think big. I have always told them all, they can do anything they put their mind to, and I want to be that influence in my granddaughter's life too. I would give anything to work on putting it behind us and rebuilding our relationship.

Liam

My third born and what a little delight. The same volume of love I had experienced before came flooding through my heart. With each birth, I had more love in my life and more love in my heart. I never imagined the capacity we have for love as mothers.

Liam was a bundle of absolute joy, and never demanding. He has a laid back personality; sometimes too laid back. He's a loving person, and when he was little he liked to be helpful. He was always affectionate and loved nothing more than a good hug and lots of attention. He was probably the most loving of the boys, although they were all loving in their own ways. We went through a difficult time with Liam's grandmother who decided she wanted custody of him. After a long, painful, and stressful battle, I lost full custody of him. This was difficult for me. I missed him terribly. However, it gave us a unique relationship and bond. We talked a lot whenever it was possible, and when he was with me, I gave him all of my attention and love. I probably overcompensated way too much because of the guilt I felt for him not being with his brothers and me all the time. And in many ways, I spoiled him and let him get away with more than he should have.

We have always had a good relationship, and despite some bumps along the way we still do.

Liam is a highly intelligent person, and I love the conversations we have. He is passionate about the world we live in. The environment and human suffering are his most significant concerns. He is vocal and very opinionated, straightforward, and not afraid to go against the grain. His knowledge and viewpoint blow me away at times; he never ceases to amaze me. He is his own person, something I really admire about him. He doesn't care what anyone thinks of him; he is comfortable with who he is, and I'm very proud of that. He has dreadlocks, wears ethical clothing, and is mindful of what he eats. You could say he's a bit of a modern-day hippy. He is such a gentle soul, however, he can turn on you if you attempt to abuse him. He's like a gentle giant, a soft soul with a calm demeanour.

I love him deeply, and I miss him so much. I am so looking forward to watching him grow and witnessing the difference he will make in this world. I have no doubt that he will accomplish amazing things. His passion is immense and when he channels it in the right direction it will be so powerful. I'm not sure if he wants to be a dad; however, I know he would be an amazing one. I look forward to his future, whatever that might be.

CC

I always wanted a girl every time I got pregnant, and it was no secret. I wanted to have the same relationship I had with my mum with her. I believe I manifested her in my life; the visions I kept having of the little girl before I was pregnant look exactly like her. I would never need any proof that I can create anything I put my mind to again.

My pregnancy with her is the only one where I found out the sex and went for private scans. As soon as I reached sixteen weeks in my pregnancy, I had a scan to find out the sex. After almost twenty-two years, I was finally getting my girl, and she was so worth the wait. That same night I found out about my daughter, I went for a soak in the bath. I went, I told her dad I'm going to spend some quality time with my daughter. I stayed in that bath for a long time, singing loudly and replaying, "Make You Feel my Love," (the Adele version) over and over. From that moment on, my life became all about making her feel my love. It's important that I have quality time with my daughter and build a relationship with her that will be strong until my last breath.

She is the most caring, kind, and loving person that could have ever blessed my life. She blows my mind with how intelligent she is. Her compassion and understanding of others is awe-inspiring. The love I receive from her fills me up every day. The love I feel when I hold her makes my heart burst. We have a bond that is unbreakable and special. Our energy is very much in sync; we completely understand each other. I adore spending time with her, and it doesn't matter what we are doing. We have so much fun, and the conversations are beautiful. She is a little powerhouse. She knows her own mind, and she isn't afraid to tell you how she feels. I wonder where she gets that from. She is her mother's daughter. She is stunning and has such beauty inside and out. Every time I look at her, my heart melts with pride. She is my heart, my soul, and my life.

I'm very open with her and I consult her about what she thinks before I make many decisions, including business decisions. She is confident, polite, incredibly well behaved, and elegant. She can hold a conversation in any situation, and I never have to worry about taking her anywhere. She is a part of everything I do. She comes to events and meetings with me. Her middle name forms part of my skincare brand and will become the brand name for my children's range. We are a team, and she is my little hero. She has healed me in many ways and made me want to show up differently in this world.

I often say if I had her first, I wouldn't have had any more children, and it's also the reason I will never have more. That has nothing to do with the love I have for my sons. I wouldn't change having them for the world. However, I do love the dynamic I have with just her and me now. A mother-daughter love is very different from that of a mother and son; my entire existence is now worthwhile. My life is complete. I am beyond excited to see the amazing woman I know she will become, and I cannot wait to see everything she achieves in her life. Look out world!

* * *

I have never regretted becoming a mother so young, and certainly didn't realise that the love you can feel for another human could be so life changing. I have most definitely learned that as much as some aspects of motherhood may come naturally, having a womb is not a guarantee that you will be the perfect mother. There's no manual. A lot of the time we are doing the best we can with what we have in any given moment, including our capacity to love. You can do everything in your power to be the best parent in the world with every good intention possible and there will always be mistakes. We are only human. Making mistakes is how we learn. With the best will possible our actions and our intentions don't always yield the best results. All you can do is raise them as healthy, emotionally intelligent, balanced human beings and encourage them to lead the best life they can, the best way you can. My biggest lesson about being a mother and from life, for that matter, is that you can do many things. We are all as powerful as we want to be. No matter how much knowledge, intelligence, or wisdom you have, you can't make another person do something they don't want to. You also can't make them listen. You can only guide, advise, encourage, and love as much as necessary; the rest is up to them.

I don't know you yet, but I love you still.

Chapter 18
Raising four children alone

I love standing on my own two feet and doing things for myself. It gives me a sense of pride and strength, and you get to know yourself well. It wasn't always that way though; there have been times in my life that I have found it extremely difficult and times when I have thrived in it. I'm going to split this chapter into two parts, and you will notice where I wasn't coping and where I was succeeding.

I raised my boys alone for almost thirteen years, and for the most part, I did well on my own. There were times, where I didn't do well and that was when my life was in chaos and usually had something to do with my unhealthy family of origin or lack of money. I didn't do well in either of these two situations. The chaos with my family always had an impact on me emotionally; mainly due to me holding onto the latest incident and (unknowingly) allowing myself to be a victim of it.

Whenever I experienced a lack of funds it threw me into complete turmoil inside. I would obsess over having enough money. I had a drive to provide more for my boys than was possible at times or more than I needed to.

I was obsessed with having more, doing better, giving everything I could to them, and providing them experiences that would allow them to see how much they could achieve. I put myself and them through a lot in the process. I was so driven by wanting to have a perfect life and giving them more, I was often blind to the mistakes I was making. I made a lot of errors, and although they came from the best intentions, they also caused a lot of stress and upheaval at times. I did whatever it took to provide for my sons. I often overextended my finances to make our life better. I couldn't see that sometimes it didn't make our life better at all. I thought as long as I stayed strong and fixed whatever mistake I made and never gave up, it was okay.

Our life was a balance of fantastic experiences and stressful mistakes—ones that cost me my home on several occasions. We lived in expensive houses in good neighbourhoods and I couldn't juggle finances all the time. I thought I was doing the right thing. I thought I could make it work every time. We travelled to a lot of countries on holidays that I couldn't afford, but I wanted my sons to have what I didn't have growing up. I wanted them to see the world and know the world was a wondrous place. I wanted to expand their minds and their experience of life. In doing this, I put myself under constant stress and placed them in situations they shouldn't have had to deal with. I couldn't see that if I simply took a step back and reigned a few things in, we would have been better off overall. I was so caught up in giving them everything I could, and I didn't care what I had to put myself through to do it. There were a few incidents where I was offered the opportunity to use credit cards that had been obtained in other peoples' names. I didn't personally apply for the cards, and I'm not excusing my actions either. I took the opportunity to use them. Some people I knew who were in the business of fraud needed a female who looked respectable enough to use the cards. They got what they wanted from each of the cards, and I got what I wanted too.

I took my sons shopping and let them get whatever they wanted. I also deposited false checks into two of my bank accounts, withdrew the money, and then closed the account before the check bounced. I can't tell you how they got the checks or how the scam worked. I do know I was so driven to maintain our lifestyle that I even resorted to things I'm not proud of. As much as we lived in a good neighbourhood and my sons went to school with friends whose parents were lawyers and doctors I was a single mum struggling to get by and I was acquainted with the kind of contacts that gave me a way sometimes to take the pressure off or to give my boys more. Coupled with my constant drive to give my sons a life to rival their friends, lack of money caused such anxiety and turmoil in me that I had to do just about anything I could to calm it. I didn't have anyone I could go to for help with money. In fact, everyone else always came to me, which was an added factor.

I'm not proud of what I did, and I take full responsibility for my actions. I've been harder on myself over the years than anyone else could be, and I repeatedly beat myself up for my choices. I wasn't proud of the reflection looking at me in the mirror no matter how hard I tried or how good I thought my intentions were, and I knew I had to change it. I am proud of who I am now, and have forgiven myself because I was doing my best with what I had at that time. If I could have learned my mistakes much sooner and found a way out of my cycle quicker, I would have. I can't change any of it; all I can do is learn and make better choices.

My life now is far removed from that stressful, chaotic life as a young mother. It's just my daughter and me now. I've learned to curb the drive to provide so much that put us in unnecessary situations. My life has improved dramatically because I have learned from my past mistakes. I don't overextend financial obligations, and in many ways, I live a much simpler life. I'm able to do this because I've come through the complexities of life, and I have worked on myself enough to know what is essential and what is not. I no longer need the feel-good factor that a lot of my financial decisions were previously born from. I didn't love myself back then, and I sure as hell wasn't proud of my choices. I have learned to love myself deeply now and accept the dark and the light. I learned that it is far more valuable to have a stress free, simple, loving and joyful life than to have material things. I can raise my daughter now the way I always wanted to raise my sons. I am thankful that I made my mistakes and I am grateful I have been able to learn enough from them to know how to bring her up in a stable environment based on love and encouragement to achieve. I never forget that my circumstances are very different now, and I don't take away any of the responsibility for all of the pain I caused my sons. However, I take credit for always trying, never giving up, continuously growing, and still having the best intentions at heart.

I have messed up big time, I have learned, and I have adjusted my actions accordingly. I can never change the past, but I can change the future. I put all my energy into doing better now; my drive is to give back and make a difference with my lessons. Take ownership of your past; it's the best thing you will ever do for yourself and everyone else.

I don't know you yet, but I love you still.

Chapter 19
Not Knowing My Granddaughter From Birth

I never imagined that I would find myself in the position of not sharing in the joy of having a grandchild, especially with my son Michael. I thought Michael and I would be close forever, until one day quite literally he wasn't there.

I woke up to find my front door to the house slightly open and him gone along with all of his things. There had been a lot of tension between us regarding his girlfriend at the time, my granddaughter's mother. We didn't see eye to eye, but I never imagined he would just leave like that. I went after him of course, and I didn't behave the way I should have. I was out of my mind actually and I accept full responsibility for that. He didn't speak to me for five years after that and things are still fractured even now.

I can't explain what it's like to suddenly lose your son like that. For me it was heartbreaking. It's hard to accept that a child you raised all alone and tried your best to give everything to, cut you out of his life. About a year after Michael left home, my son Liam shared the news that Michael was going to have a child and I was going to be a grandmother. Finding out you are going to have a grandchild is meant to be joyful and exciting. I felt I had that taken away from me, and my heart was breaking so badly that I shut it out and pretended it wasn't happening. Michael didn't tell me when she was born, and I wasn't allowed to go see her. I contacted him when I was given the news to congratulate him and tried to express that I hoped he would understand what the challenges of being a parent and how much you put into a child. He took offense to that and shut me out once more.

I didn't see my granddaughter until she was almost five years old. It was the strangest feeling. This beautiful little person that was part of me, yet a stranger, a child I didn't know at all. I wanted to hug her and tell her I loved her, but she didn't know me and I didn't know her. The first time I held my granddaughter, it was a quick hug with my mind firmly focused on not making her feel uncomfortable. I was excited and nervous all at the same time; on eggshells the whole time, making sure I didn't say anything that would spoil the moment or get me cut out again. When we were saying our goodbyes, I had to focus all of my mind on not breaking down like some crazy woman in front of this child didn't know. I haven't seen her since then and I still tread carefully with my son. Sometimes he speaks to me and sometimes he doesn't. I send him messages without expectation now. I've learned it's too painful to do anything else.

I would love to have a proper relationship with my granddaughter, and I will never give up hope of recovering a good relationship with my son and making up for lost time with my granddaughter.

Never give up on anyone you love if it is worth fixing. Sometimes, it isn't worth repairing, and you have to be willing to see the difference.

I don't know you yet, but I love you still.

Chapter 20
Father or Not

When I planned this book, I decided I was going to add this chapter about feeling like my father never cared for me or much else. Then I began to question if it was relevant or deserved space. However, I am human, and I can't write a book about baring it all if I'm not fully prepared to do so myself. So perhaps this chapter is really about vulnerability and accepting our dark and our light. I received a lot of light from my mother for which I am forever grateful, and I have received a lot of dark from my father, for which I am thankful, nonetheless. It creates balance and a certain amount of self-awareness of my own dark and light.

I see life as a series of experiences you unpack and learn from. And my relationship, or lack thereof, with my father is certainly something I've had to unpack. It's a strange experience to explain. My father was always around growing up, but he was never really present. After my mother passed away, my father never gave any support with grief, my life, my sons when they were growing up, and now with my daughter. My daughter has only ever seen him three times, and briefly at that. He has never supported any of my business endeavours. In fact, he has always been negative and against me creating my own business.

As far as love goes, this is something I never really felt from him as a child nor as an adult. We only talk when I contact him, and I only see him if I go to his house. I do not get a call for my birthday, or for Christmas or New Year, and my children don't get any care or support from him either. This is a relationship that, in the past, caused me a lot of pain and anger. I had to do some deep inner work on this one. It is a relationship that I had to make a choice to emotionally remove from my life and one I'm happy I've made peace with. It's no better or worse than it is; it just is.

I've come to see his role in my life as one that prepared me to deal with any form of negativity from anyone. No one else's negative feedback or attempts at dragging me down can ever be more than a mild irritation and a push to keep shining my light. When you have gotten used to the constant criticism that I have endured from inside of my family it toughens you up to the outside world. It makes you have to develop your own opinion of yourself that is strong, loving, and unwavering in order to keep emerging as the bright beaming light that you were always born to be.

For a lot of years, I tried to work at this relationship and I caused myself a lot of pain in doing so. I felt angry that he doesn't love me or care about my life and it made me feel unimportant. That feeling of unimportance is a feeling that hung over me and resurfaced in many situations that didn't serve me or my life one bit. Those negative emotions caused a lot of pain in my life and affected a lot of my emotional wellbeing, my relationships, and how I dealt with various situations for many years.

If you have any kind of relationship in your life that is negative and causes you pain, I urge you to do the inner work to heal yourself and have the courage to choose to emotionally remove yourself. Love yourself first. I wish I learned this much earlier. My healing really took flight when I learned to fall deeply in love with myself, the dark and the light. By accepting the dark, I was able to see just how beautiful the light is.

I now see my father's role in my life as the one that was meant to try to hold me back in order for my true self to break through and reveal who I was born to be. We are all born with a meant-to-be-ism, the gifts that we are meant to share with the world. The person we were meant to be isn't something that we inherited from our parents, nor is it something we gain from society. We were born with it. It's always been inside of you. Do you have a minute to just be? Not as you think it should be, but as it is meant to be. There is something inside of you that's meant to be.

Acceptance of oneself and acceptance of others is key.

I don't know you, but I love you still. Smile and love yourself.

CHAPTER 21
ALWAYS FEELING ALONE

And

Discovering I Never Truly Was

For nearly my entire adult life I have felt alone. It's no surprise to me now looking back. I'm sure it won't be for you either now that you understand what happened in my early years. It stems from the childhood sexual abuse, almost dying, and the significant losses I suffered.

I caused myself so much heartache and pain. I did this by not dealing with my own emotional healing and pretending to myself and the world around me I was okay. I also never acknowledged to myself that I feared being left each time I got close to someone or let them into my world.

I now know I imposed a large amount of those feelings on myself and in some ways deep down I never really let anyone close enough to me for them to be there for me. My friendships and relationships were generally with people who were mostly emotionally unavailable; a pattern that took me a long time to recognise.

My young adulthood was shadowed by a lot of pain and heartaches that I didn't know how to deal with, nor did I have the chance to. I had just lost the two most important and significant women in my life. Love and happiness seemed like it wasn't meant for me. I was a nineteen-year-old single mum with a two-year-old to take care of and a family that completely imploded. I had a great deal of responsibility and not much else. It was a lot to handle, and I did what I do best—get on with it.

Subconsciously, I had chosen a path which meant I could feel secure, but not cared for or loved. I spent much of my adulthood giving to people. I failed to recognise I could never receive love or support properly from anyone because I was focused on providing all the time in the hope I would get that same level in return. The problem was, the more I gave the more I felt I wasn't getting enough back. But no one could have ever given enough or measured up to my giving because I didn't love myself enough to receive love properly from anyone or even to recognise it as sufficient. The story I had learned or was certainly telling myself was that I wasn't meant to be loved properly, I wasn't good enough, and I didn't deserve true happiness or a proper loving family. When I am close to people they either hurt me or leave me. If I kept giving more love, generosity, understanding, and tolerance I would somehow become enough and be worthy of love, happiness, and the people in my life who were truly there for me. Of course, what happens is the complete opposite because we are operating from such low vibrating energy that we don't attract the right people into our life.

How can you break the cycle? Self-love—truly finding love for who you are inside and that includes the obvious beauty but also the unique edges and imperfections. Cherish and adore yourself more than anyone else ever could. True acceptance of self and being completely unapologetically you is one of the best decisions you'll ever make for yourself. Once I learned to truly love myself, and more importantly, accept myself and step into being all of me, my whole world opened up. I began to see a whole new me and how powerful, reliable, and capable I am and how much capacity I have for loving other people deeply. Self-love is not just about you; it's about everyone around you. When you love yourself enough, when you give yourself enough, and when you know how important you are and how you show up in this world, no one can ever take it from you. Your capacity to give to the world around you grows with every act of love and kindness you give to yourself.

Although it may be one of the most challenging journeys of self-discovery you will ever embark on, I can assure you it is worth it and will be your greatest love and greatest ally. Suddenly the world is brighter, the grass is a whole new shade of green, the sky is the most vivid blue even on a cloudy day, your step springs for no reason at all, but most of all you can't help but shine and spread love.

I encourage you to be loving with everyone, even the stranger you meet on the street. However, I encourage you to be the most devoted being you can possibly be with yourself first and foremost. It will change your life in ways you can never have imagined possible.

I don't know most of you yet, but I can say I already love you. You are loved and adored always; it's right there inside you.

Chapter 22
Being Strong And Finding Strength Is The Same

To find strength and to be strong is the same. You first need to be strong to find your strength, and you need strength to be strong.

I have learned in life that even seemingly strong people need to find strength and those who don't think they are strong have strength. We have it inside us. In fact, we have everything we need inside us. We just have to reclaim our power to access it.

People always ask me how I stay so strong. They wonder how I could have endured everything I've gone through in my life. I suppose I had to. I was meant to. My mum always said what is meant for you will never go past you. I know she did not foresee the struggles I have had, but she was right. We get in life what we attract the most. I have had turbulence in my life that meant I had to be strong. I am able to find more strength each time because I've had more time flexing that muscle than most and I'm also a savage inside. I want to thrive so bad that I feed that savage every day. I let her free to gorge as much as she likes. She is wild and free, and she comes out whenever I need her.

You have the strength you need, too. You are a strong person and you have that savage inside of you too. He or she will help you experience what you have to and what you are meant to if you just feed it and let it free.

Oh, and just because you're strong doesn't mean you don't need support. It doesn't mean you can't ask for help. Seeking help actually makes you stronger. You have to have strength to ask for help when you're strong so go ahead and flex that muscle. I've also learned that even when you don't think you are strong; you will find strength in asking for help. So go find your strength.

We are all strong, we all have strength, and we all have everything we need inside of us. We all have our savage inside of us if we need it enough. I know you have it inside, you know you have it inside you, now it's time to set him or her free.

I don't know you yet, but I love you still.

CHAPTER 23
MYSELF FIRST

After losing my nana and my mum I developed some pretty destructive insecurities—never feeling important or loved enough. And it was a big problem in my life for years. It was slowly eating me alive. Of course, I didn't realise this while I was going through it. It was only after years of thinking it was everyone else who was the problem and being a victim to it that I finally began to see this pattern. I finally unpacked it and realised I never felt important to anyone because I wasn't making myself important to me. I didn't love myself.

Sure, there was plenty of evidence to support my feelings of never being important enough or loved enough. That insecurity wasn't born from nothing. The more evidence I gathered the less important or loved I felt and the cycle continued on and on. I was always looking for proof I was important or valued or loved me enough by someone. I was giving away too much of myself in an attempt to feel what I thought I needed in return. When we are a prey to this insecurity or mindset, we are in a constant battle within.

You stay in a constant cycle of never feeling enough or loved. It's not because the people around you have bad intentions (most of them). It's because you made it easy for them. You never put yourself first or made yourself important enough. So why would they do that for you? You don't love yourself enough, so you will never feel enough love from anyone, whether they were giving it or not. When you don't love yourself inside and out, don't put your needs first, or value yourself, you will always search for that from other people. It's not missing from you, it's inside of you. It is not something that will ever come from someone else. It has to come from inside you first, and then it will radiate out to everyone else. You will attract those kinds of loving people into your life.

If you don't learn to fall deeply in love with yourself, value yourself, and put your needs above all else you will continue to attract people who take what you are willing to give while they provide the bare minimum in return (or at least that's how it will feel). They can only give so much because they don't love themselves either. You accept that because you don't value yourself enough, and they don't value themselves either. They don't make you important because you don't value yourself enough. They don't feel valuable either so they can't give that to you. You are two half people operating from the outside in trying to become whole by getting what you need from the other person. It doesn't work. I have tried and tried.

No one can make you feel loved, valuable, or enough. You have to be in love with yourself and important to you, and then you will know deep down that you are enough. It all comes from within, and when you make yourself whole, you will start to attract other people who are whole. When you are operating from within, you are sending those messages and vibrations out into the world. Those who aren't vibrating at that level will not be able to handle it, and something will repel you or them. Anyone who is operating at that level will be drawn to you like a magnet. Just as we attract like-minded people, we also invite the people who are on the same energy level. "Love and above," as I call it. Love and above is when you are operating from the love you have for yourself first, then the love you have to give. When you are vibrating on this level, your love is so much more powerful, and you can give it fully because you never worry about getting it back.

If I can inspire or teach you anything from this entire book I wish for you to learn to love yourself. Do whatever work is required for you to do so. I want you to unpack whatever baggage you need so you can fill yourself up with love. It might be a lot—it was for me—but you need to keep unpacking it every day. It might even be painful. It will mean you have to look at yourself and be willing to take responsibility for your part in every unpleasant situation you have been in. The reward is incredible. Accept yourself; both the light and the dark. Without dark, there is no light. Love yourself unconditionally, completely, and joyfully. Be unapologetic with your love for yourself. Those who aren't operating on that level will call you selfish. They will say you think you are better than them. They will say you think too highly of yourself. They will assume your standards are too high. When other people aren't operating from a place of self-love, they will try to tear you down. That's where they are comfortable and it's much less effort to tear you down than to work on themselves and come up to your level. They aren't bad people; they just aren't your people.

The best thing I ever did was give myself permission to do the work, and learn to fall deeply in love with myself, put myself first, and make myself the most critical person in my world. There's an unwavering belief that I am enough. I'm happier than I have ever been and now there are so many people in my life who love me for who I am. There's a tattoo on my arm that says, "I am enough," with two love hearts in the infinity shape. That symbolises I am enough for me, and I am enough for anyone else. It also signifies that my love for myself and the love I give is infinite. It is always flowing in and out; it will always come back to me. It's a constant reminder, just in case I slip. It's a daily practice.

Give yourself permission to do the work needed to love yourself and want what you want. Remember when you had to get a permission slip from your parents to do things in school? Write your own bloody permission slip. And I mean write one if that is what it takes. Write as many as you need and put them everywhere, so it will continuously remind you until it becomes second nature. You don't ever need anyone to give you a permission slip, or give you love or to make you feel vital again. Give it all to yourself first, you are the only person that needs to provide you with anything. Put yourself first, set your standards and don't settle for less, make what you want the most important thing to you, learn to fall deeply in love with yourself including all your edges and imperfections and don't ever apologise for it, being authentically truly you or wanting what you want. You will be happier than you have ever been, you will know deep in your core you are enough, and your people will find you.

Be you, be all of you and love yourself so bloody deeply while you're doing it. It will bring the most healing transformation that you could give to yourself. You are always enough.

I don't know you yet, but I love you still.

Chapter 24
No Mask to Hide Behind, The Freedom of Vulnerability and The Courage to Own It All

It's no secret among those that know me that I am who I say I am and I show up in this world exactly as I am. I am raw, blunt at times, intense, passionate, giving, strong, and I own who I am. I live with a huge purpose, but most of all I am loving. I hope *Rebel Woman* will challenge your ideas, your thoughts and your feelings. Challenge how you view Self and how you view the world. It all comes from a very deep place that is fueled by a pure desire to thrive and make a difference.

I see my life as a series of events and lessons that I have endured so that I can share them in order to help prevent you from making some (or all, of the experiences I have had, wouldn't that be amazing) highly unlikely but it's a good thought, right?

There are things in this book that may have shocked you to the core, brought you to tears, inspired you, made you angry and moved you in ways you never expected. I would be surprised if some things haven't made you question me and the world we live in. Let yourself feel all of that, not to feel them for me, for you. Picture yourself in every single one of these events and make an internal personal commitment that you will set your standard for yourself high and you will never waiver from it. Feel it deeply? Be so moved you take your life by the horns, create whatever your heart desires and do it right now.

I shared these selected series of events for good reason, it's my way of owning my life and encouraging you to do it too, it's so bloody freeing. All of my mistakes laid bare for you to learn from, don't learn my lessons, take what you want from this and learn what's relevant to you. There is so much we can endure in our life if we allow it, but we can come through so much more than we ever thought possible. There is so much beauty and love, and it's always there waiting for you, you just have to be open to it and look for it. We live in a wondrous world and we can create our life to be whatever we want it to be, we just have to want it enough. We have to love ourselves deeply enough to give ourselves permission to fly. We don't need to be a victim of our circumstances, we can take ownership of them, own your part in every bit of suffering and own your life every day.

I'm unapologetically me, it's in everything I do, it's who I am deep inside, I actually really like being vulnerable and putting all of myself out there fully, there is pure beauty in it and no one can ever hurt you or take it away because when you are truly yourself and you stand in your power no one can mess with that. It's very empowering, liberating and freeing. No mask to hide behind, nothing to hide from, I can't even hide from myself (pure freedom) being comfortable in my own skin, being comfortable with all of me, including the dark and the light (finally). I own it all and I walk with my head held high, I am proud of who I have become, I love myself deeply and I love you too.

I am determined to live on course, for me, for my family and for you, I'm passionate about sharing my story and sharing the lessons I can bring. I'm drawn to create the life I truly want and deserve, My purpose is to inspire you to realise life is happening for you and learn to harness the power and beauty that lies behind every struggle. My vision is to create a movement that co-elevates women and makes a huge difference in the world. I'm always emerging because I'm always learning and growing and moving forward (I will never stop). I'm able to turn around every negative thing in my life, everything, and use it for fuel and power to thrive and I know you can too.

I hope by now you are starting to see that you have everything you need already inside of you, go take your world, take flight and soar high, smile and rise, smile and rise. Collect your power, take back self and own it all. (like I know you can)

I love you.

Chapter 25
Desire to dream and achieve

I have always been a dreamer, I hope you can see that my desire to achieve has always been a driving force for me. Although I didn't always take the right approach, the passion and the intention remained the same. I wanted to create a life worth living, full of rich experiences for myself and my children. Throughout my life, I managed to achieve certain levels of success, but breaking the ceiling was a challenge. Until I healed myself and learned to fall deeply in love with myself.

At that turning point, my entire life just opened up before my eyes, the sky was now bright blue, even on a cloudy day. The grass was a shade of green I never noticed until then, and I felt peace and joy like never before. The pivotal element in where I am now and where I am going, was when I stepped into myself fully, putting myself out there like never before. Being raw, vulnerable, sharing myself and my story with anyone who needs to hear it. Not hiding from myself, not keeping this extraordinary person locked away from everyone, including me. Being more me, than I've ever been before and not being afraid of who I truly am or what I ultimately bring to the world. No fear of what I want, going after it all, including in my personal life and doing the things I very much desire. Most importantly, feeling the way I desire every moment of every day, and it is scheduled into everything I do.

It is also the reason I finally began to learn to fly. I have always had a fascination with small aeroplanes, and I had always wanted to learn to fly. I was afraid deep down, I wouldn't be good at it, so I continued to dream. When I finally got the courage to try, it was everything I ever imagined it would be and more. The feeling of being in control of an aircraft was just beyond anything I had ever felt. I found out during my first lesson, it was something I was excellent at, it felt so natural to me, and I wasn't afraid anymore. The instructor told me I was a natural, which just confirmed what I was feeling already. I loved it so much I had forgotten the fear I felt. My first ever lesson and the instructor felt confident enough to let me fly the plane in a straight angle of attack until the aircraft stalled and began to freefall. What a rush of adrenalin and total freedom, I knew right then I had to train for a private pilot licence. The peace of mind and the freedom I feel when I fly isn't like anything else I have ever felt. Only those who fly, know why birds sing. Spending time at the airfield and flying became a big part of my stepping into myself and certainly beats any other form of stress relief I've ever known. I plan to have my own aeroplane and spend as much time flying as I can.

If you have the desire to do something personal that serves you in ways you know will be greatly beneficial, do it today. Don't let fear hold you back from anything you desire. You will never regret it, everything you could ever desire is on the other side of fear.

Some of these messages may be overlapping themselves, that is deliberate. It is only through repetition we learn, my entire life is a testament to that. I want these messages to be so familiar that it feels like they are part of you. They were always in you, I just need you to remember them. Everything you need is already inside of you, I'm only here to help bring it forward into existence. Set your champion free, she is extraordinary.

I don't know you yet; but I love you still.

CHAPTER 26
MY BUSINESS LIFE

(where it began and where it is now)

This may be quite a surprise to you considering the complexities of my story at times, but I have had a business life since I left college at eighteen. When I first started my journey in business, I had a business admin service. However, my entrepreneurial spirit and talent were born much earlier. From the age of ten, in fact, I began to decide I wanted more from life.

I would do anything to make money, and of course, this is where my cycle of using achievement and drive began. Each and every time, there was an emotional discomfort in my life I pushed myself harder to achieve.

At ten, I would sweep and wash stairs for my nana and other neighbours who would pay me. I would go to the store for older people, help with chores, anything that got me some pocket money. I then started a paper round, delivering evening newspapers after school during the week and delivering Sunday newspapers. There was an older girl that lived across the street from me, and she had a much better Sunday round than I did. She also didn't like doing it, so I bought it from her. I was thirteen at that time, my first business purchase. I paid £53, roughly what she would have made in six months. I knew I could make more money. Her round was in a new estate of private houses, and they were still building more. I could get more customers and grow it, I would also get more tips. Every time new people moved into new houses, I would go offer to deliver their newspapers. I built it up so much it started to become challenging to handle, and I didn't really enjoy it that much anymore. I decided the sensible thing was to sell it.

After my business admin service, I became an aerobics instructor and set up my own classes called Fit 4 Life, I loved it. I would rent out community centres and church halls. It gave me all the freedom I needed with my boys. I decided I wanted more than that, so I went to University to study Law. During that time, I was asked to help an acquaintance with his business, and I became a partner. We worked with less fortunate boys who had been thrown out of school, teaching them to use the discipline from Basketball in everyday life. I was the person responsible for getting the clients and projects. Our partnership didn't go so well despite how well business was going, and we parted ways. I went to all of the clients we had in person and pitched a concept I had for working with girls, and every single client brought me on board.

I put together lesson plans and project outcomes and submitted applications for grants of government funding that I was granted. The project was named, Fit 4 Life, based on the same principles of discipline and respect but teaching beauty and getting these girls back into education. I had eighty-four per cent success rate with that project, and it is something I am immensely proud of. The secret to the success of that project, love and respect. I loved those girls, at the start of every new group I would pick the one with the most attitude. I would ask her to put her hand out, and when she did, I would motion like I was putting something in her hand. I would say, that is my respect, and I would close her hand. I then said if you chose to keep my respect, I will do everything I can for you and every promise I make I will keep, even if I have to bend over backwards to make it happen. If you don't, I can't help you. Not one of those girls let themselves down. In many cases, I was the first person in their life that held space for them, saw them and heard them clearly. I gave them every bit of my respect because I could see myself in each and every one of them.

Yearning to be seen, longing to be heard and longing to be loved for who they were. I am proud, and I am thankful I was able to give them that for the short six weeks they were with me. Eighty-four per cent of them got back into education and stayed there. I also saved one girl from a drug overdose, her cousin contacted me late one night, she had been missing for two days, we went looking for her and found her in another cousins house slumped in a chair. Called an ambulance and got her to hospital, thankfully they pumped her stomach. When she woke up she told me I should have left her there, I shouldn't have saved her, she didn't want to live. She was so angry at me, something I was really prepared for. I told her she could be mad with me for as long as she needed to be, but I was glad I saved her and I would do it over and over again. She cried and hugged me and we both cried, of course. That will stay with me until the day I stop breathing. I couldn't understand how much she must have been through to be feeling that at fifteen years old. I knew her story, but knowing her story doesn't mean I knew her and what she had actually been through.

I travelled back and forth to Beijing to train for massage and after a year of training, I started my salon, Qi. It is pronounced Chee, and it means energy in Chinese. I rented a Victorian building over three floors and renovated it all, I put all of my finances into that business, which caused a lot of my financial struggles and my decisions to resort to my less than sensible or legal ways of getting money at times. No matter how much I tried, that business just wasn't making a profit. It just wasn't the right location, and it wasn't the right time either. I loved it though, amongst all of the turbulence in my life this was my safe place, it gave me a sense of pride, a sense of achievement. I had the keys to the front door, it was my business, and I had done it all from nothing. Ultimately I had to come to terms with the fact that it wasn't going to work, I couldn't achieve what I wanted.

That was also when we moved away, I put the entire contents of my business and my home into one big van and left the North East for good. We moved to Northamptonshire, and I quickly set about getting my business going again. I began doing hen parties for a party planning company, added treatment packages for hotels in Milton Keynes and before long, I had a thriving business again. I was well known around the area, and I was very active in the business community. We moved from Northampton to Milton Keynes, and I then opened up a new salon. The salon I lost when I went to prison.

After my past caught up with me and I had my little holiday, I set up again in the shopping mall in Milton Keynes. A challenging location, with very high overheads and the added pressure of the community knowing my story. I ran that salon for eighteen months and worked seven days per week, and I just couldn't break even. I had also been living in shared accommodation with my sons to try to make ends meet before moving in with my daughter's father. The choice to keep fighting to make it work was taken away, four days before my daughter was born, when I received a call from the centre manager telling me they had locked my unit up and I shouldn't come to work. Three days after my daughter was born, her father collected all of my furniture and equipment from the salon. I was devastated, but I had a baby to think about and a collapsed pelvis to recover from.

One year later, I set back up in a space I rented from a well-known health club, it built quickly, and I then moved to a converted barn. It was at that point Manor Grove Spa was born, and the emphasis was very much retreat and relaxation. The business grew fast, and I very quickly outgrew those premises. I moved to a bigger converted barn my landlord at that time had. The company was thriving, and so was I now.

I decided I wanted to launch my skincare brand, so I closed the spa. I had already begun with massage candles within the spa, and I wanted to develop a full range of products. Elise Marques London was born and is still going today.

Now to the present day, where I run EML and Michelle Margaret Marques Coaching. *Rebel Woman* events, workshops and international speaking engagements. I am working on the Rebel Universe foundation and there is a whole lot more to come.

I have learned most of all, never ever give up, don't let go of your dreams and desires no matter what. Just keep getting back up, dust yourself off and try another way. Or get up, dress up and bloody show up as I like to say. Everything you were born to be is inside you, what are you waiting for? Be more you than you've ever been before, from that place you can create extraordinary things.

I don't know you yet, but I love you still.

CHAPTER 27
MY MISSION

Realising that I don't just want to run a business, I want to start a movement has been another pivotal breakthrough. I want to give back in every way possible. I am passionate about helping women create the impossible, celebrating, elevating, holding space for other women and helping girls become empowered women. It's the very reason I wrote this book, and I am building the Rebel Universe mission brand and foundation.

I am committed to creating a movement where women come together in support of each other, a safe space where we can heal our wounds and co-create our dreams. A place where we are not available for limits or fears. I have seen firsthand the magic that happens when women come together to share knowledge, support, understanding, care, skills and passions. It is profoundly transformative. My biggest wish is *Rebel Woman*, becomes a place where you can return time after time to connect deeply with yourself and others in this meaningful way.

I aspire for this to be a space for you to be seen, heard, loved and acknowledged in the complexities of who you are. To learn tangible skills, gain valuable knowledge and to build lasting relationships that grow into business partnerships, mentorships and life-long friendships. I intend to help women who want to create the life they absolutely wish to, women who want to truly impact and change the world.

I am on a mission to pay forward inspiration, wisdom and knowledge to millions of women. Inspiring them to capture the human experience, take back Self, have the courage to own it all and emerge with life happening for them, no matter where they are on the journey now. My passion is to do this through collective reach, and I need your help too.

Every book has the potential to change lives. My invitation is that you write a personal note and then pass the book on to another woman. Imagine the ripple effect we will co-create together by passing this book on to someone you know it will impact and then she passes it on and so on and so on?

I have a beautiful vision of the book being passed on to so many women, that it becomes worn in a rather comforting way from all the milage and notes that have to be stapled into it because there's no space left to write. It becomes infused with the energy and experience of all who have read it before, which in turn transforms it into a beautifully powerful love letter of feminine connection, co-elevation ownership and inspiration...

I don't know you yet, but I love you still.

Chapter 28
Delicious discovery year

I cannot express or impress upon you thoroughly enough what an adventure CC and I have had this year thus far. And it's not over as I sit here writing this chapter. In January 2019 I made the decision that this was going to be our best year yet, we were going to go on a big adventure. CC and I came up with the idea of a delicious discovery year, and I can say for sure it has most certainly been that. We left the UK on February 14th 2019, (valentines day). This was deliberate and a very bold act of love for ourselves.

New York was the first stop, and we spent three months there. I've been visiting New York for seventeen years, and I have a severe love affair with that city. I had always dreamed of moving to NYC, and I wanted to finally find out if my New York dream was real or viable. The plan was to spend three months deciding if it was the right move for us permanently. It wasn't all plain sailing; however, we enjoyed the ride as much as possible anyway. Living in New York was a dream come true for me, I love the atmosphere, the energy, the people and the buildings. CC was having a different experience, while there are many aspects of NYC she loves, especially the buildings. The busyness and the hustle and bustle was not something she enjoyed at all. We spent time in different areas, upstate NY, New Jersey, in the heart of Manhattan and in Forest Hills Queens, which became our favourite. We really enjoyed the uniqueness of the area. The convenience of the stores, restaurants and cafes and the ease of getting in and out of the city. We met some fantastic characters along the way and experienced heartfelt and warm human kindness. Ultimately we decided New York was great to visit and a temporary hub we will always go back to, but not a permanent home.

We moved on to British Columbia in Canada where the plan remained the same, to spend some time there experiencing life. We both immediately loved it, the scenery is just stunning, and the lifestyle is definitely more our pace. We bonded with my family and had some fantastic adventures. Our visit to Whistler being our absolute favourite. It gave me a grounded place in which to finish my book. The people we have met and bonded with here will always be a beautiful part of our life. Although we initially felt very positive about setting down roots and making BC our home, we were undecided. However, we plan on visiting often, BC has a lot to offer mountains, lakes, beaches and breathtaking scenery. It's also very close to the US border, which allowed me to do some speaking in Seattle.

We made plans and arrangements to move on to Barbados, the next adventure of our delicious discovery year. I have been visiting Barbados for fifteen years, and I have friends there. I consider family. I have a special connection with the island; it felt like a second home.

I always planned to have a home there one day, from my first visit. I just fell in love with the island and its people. I love the atmosphere and the emphasis on family. What is not to love about hot sunny weather, white sandy beaches and crystal clear blue ocean. Barbados is way more than that though, it's a very nurturing place for me and I've never experienced the kind of peace I have there, anywhere else. CC is also part Barbadian, and I want her to experience that part of her background. We have made Barbados our home, although there will always be more delicious discoveries right here. There will be so much more traveling and adventures to come.

As we enjoy more adventures in our delicious discovery years. I would like you to think about what adventures you can plan for your own delicious discovery year. Make every year a delicious discovery year, expect the things you desire most and make them happen. Create the life you want, believe me, it is absolutely possible. If you can dream it, you can believe it, and if you believe it, it's already yours.

I don't know you yet, but I love you still.

Chapter 29
Becoming the Rebel Woman

COVID 19 dare I say it, is what created the space for another whole shift in me and the opportunity for me to step into more of me than I have ever been before. Rebel Woman is who I am, it's who I have always been, my whole life has led me to this point.

In mid-March, Barbados confirmed the first two cases of COVID 19 and immediately my daughter's school closed. I made a conscious decision that I was going to make the most of the time just as I had when I went to prison. Although I didn't know how long the pause was going to last. I began to focus on pivoting my coaching business and decided I needed to re-brand and change the messaging to suit my bold personality. I worked with a branding specialist who develops brands based on the strongest elements of the client's personality, through that process we found that my authentic personality is the rebel and that resonated with me very deeply. I knew it matched me completely and the story of my life.

I also enrolled in some very high-level coaching and leadership training with a master in the coaching world. This style of coaching incorporates a blend of coaching and leadership skills, this truly is fearless coaching, nothing hidden and no holding back. This fits very well with who I am, the rebel without a mask. In just four-short-months, I completed several training programs and that's when the Up-Level Rebel idea came from. I completely changed my business from a coaching practice to a leadership consultancy, changed my branding, changed my client base, and I decided I couldn't just stop there. I made the choice to change my book This Woman, first launched in September 2019 to Rebel Woman, and transform it. I also launched Rebel Universe Publishing and that is when the Rebel Universe campaign and charity fund was born.

The whole process has been inspiring and it has completely aligned my entire mission. It is also testament to how I come from my vision and effortlessly create the impossible. You must first create the highest vision and then come from that place. Create something that feels so impossible that it inspires you to take every step you need to develop, grow, move mountains, and never let anything stop you. Transforming This Woman to Rebel Woman has been freeing and has had me step into more of who I am than ever before.

Notes To My Future Self

My central vision is to continue to create delicious discovery years with my daughter. Travel is at the centre of my world, I will purchase my own aeroplane and continue to fly. Build connected relationships, community and a valued network. I will have homes in various locations so that I can always entertain, have the feeling of coming home whenever I travel and create beautiful experiences for myself and the ones I love.

Continue my movement, build my mission brand and my foundation. Develop my coaching and leadership consultancy, methodology, events, workshops, courses, programs, masterminds, retreats and other books.

Build Elise Marques London. Add a home and lifestyle range. A children's range, and a men's range.

Most of all, I will continue to hold space for women to be vulnerable. To help you all create the life you truly deserve. Be this *Rebel Woman*, no holding back, the rebel without a mask. Freely showing my vulnerability, and always courageously owning it all.

What happens next? What notes will you write to your future self? Where will your next delicious discovery year take you? What have you discovered about yourself or what you want since you began Rebel Woman? How will you transform your world? What kind of impossible will you create? How much more of you, do you want to be?

Rebel Woman is each and every one of us. She is whoever you want to be. I invite you to join this movement, discard the mask you hide behind, find freedom in vulnerability, have the courage to own it all, and always remember your vision is a place to come from, not to get to.

Here's to your future self, being more you than you've ever been before, and creating the impossible.

I don't know you yet, but I look forward to meeting you along the way.

Love and Possibilities Always

Michelle xx

THANK YOU

I want to thank every single person who is or has been part of my life. You have made the ride intense in one way or another, and I wouldn't be This Woman without the experiences you brought with you, positive, negative or neutral. I am thankful for it all, and I give love to you all.

I thank my children for all of the love, joy and tears you have brought into my life and for experiences we have shared, and will share. You are my heart, my soul and my life, and it fills me with pride to be your mum. My heart is full of gratitude and joy, and I cannot believe how lucky I am to have given birth to you all. I love you with all of my heart.

I want to thank Nancy Florence for your beautiful and heartwarming foreword you captured the essence of me and the book remarkably. I also want to thank you for all of your support, encouragement and belief, and for keeping me accountable to myself. Having you read my chapters as I wrote them was an incredible comfort and kept me going when it felt too painful. I love you.

Acknowledgements

Nancy Florence, for the personal coaching that has helped change my life and your loving friendship. Thank you, I love you.

Kat Legowik, for your support, encouragement, laughs and crazy fantastic friendship. Thank you, I love you.

Fabienne Boixel, for your support, encouragement and beautiful friendship. Thank you, I love you.

Karin Ridgers, for your support, encouragement and lovely friendship. Thank you, I love you.

Katie Webster, for your support, encouragement and continued friendship. Thank you, I love you.

Sam Johnston, for your support, encouragement and great friendship. Thank you, I love you.

Jessica Eriksson, for your support, encouragement and caring friendship. Thank you, I love you.

Rosemary Ann Moffat-Smith, for being a fantastic loving Aunt, and friend. Thank you, I love you.

John Smith, for your support, encouragement, and warm friendship. Thank you, I love you.

Kerry and Ryan, for giving me a grounded, peaceful place to finish this book. Thank you, I love you.

Credits:

Amber Newton, for your stunning photography. For the cover of the book and in the mission campaign. Thank you, I love you.

Sarah Jane Buckle, for your design wizardry, uncovering my rebel side and bringing it to my book cover. Thank you, I love you.

Josh Rivedal, for your editing talent, your meaningful encouragement and belief in me, and for bringing my voice out so much more powerfully. Thank you, I love you.

Tegan Heneke, the Director of the Rebel Voice, for putting up with the Rebel in me and all of your hard work in keeping the mission on track. Thank you, I love you.

If I haven't mentioned you here by name, please don't feel left out, I appreciate and love you still.

NOTES AND INSIGHTS

Please infuse this page with the energy and experience you had while reading *Rebel Woman*. What note will you write to the woman you are going to pass it on to, and all of the others who will gain your gift after her?

Let's co-create a beautifully powerful love letter of feminine connection, co-elevation ownership and inspiration...

NOTES AND INSIGHTS

Notes and Insights

Notes and Insights

Notes and Insights

NOTES AND INSIGHTS

Notes and Insights

Notes and Insights

Notes and Insights

NOTES AND INSIGHTS

Notes and Insights

Notes and Insights

Notes and Insights

Notes and Insights

Notes and Insights

Notes and Insights

Notes and Insights

Notes and Insights

Notes and Insights

NOTES AND INSIGHTS

Notes and Insights

Notes and Insights

Notes and Insights

Notes and Insights

Printed in Great Britain
by Amazon